THE LITTLE RED BOOK OF

HORSE WISDOM

THE LITTLE RED BOOK OF
HORSE WISDOM

Edited by Yvette Grant
Introduction by Buck Brannaman

Skyhorse Publishing

For my family, who showed me Icelandic horses with the same
generosity and enthusiasm they apply to all things.

And for Jesse, who may one day add horseback riding to the list of his
many incredible talents.

Skyhorse Publishing books may be purchased in bulk at special
discounts for sales promotion, corporate gifts, fund-raising, or
educational purposes. Special editions can also be created to
specifications. For details, contact the Special Sales Department,
Skyhorse Publishing, 307 West 36th Street, 11th Floor,
New York, NY 10018 or info@skyhorsepublishing.com.

Skyhorse® and Skyhorse Publishing® are registered trademarks of
Skyhorse Publishing, Inc.®, a Delaware corporation.
Visit our website at www.skyhorsepublishing.com

10 9 8 7 6 5 4 3 2 1

Library of Congress Cataloging-in-Publication Data is available on file.
ISBN 978-1-61608-707-4

Printed in China

Contents

Introduction

People often say the American West was tamed by brave pioneers. That's partly true, but without their horses, those pioneers might still be "on their way"!

As the only available form of transportation on land in America for hundreds of years, the horse formed an ancient bond and a fragile alliance with the human, and the human with the horse.

That human was often the "Cowboy." His role developed out of the need for skilled horsemen and stockmen to tend the vast herds of cattle in North America. There have been Cowboys all around the world who have honed their skills despite great danger to themselves. Nowadays, "Cowboy" is a term that's often used derisively. But it's a shame everyone doesn't have a chance to experience the thrill of a newborn calf taking its first breath because a Cowboy had the skill to pen the cow and pull the calf—or even do a caesarean in a pasture with only a horse, a saddle, a rope, and some primitive operating instruments, managing to save two lives at the risk of his own.

Anyway, I hope you see how ignorant it is to use the term "Cowboy" with contempt.

Looking around today, we see that the horse is used for many purposes, including ranch work, dressage, jumping, reining, cutting, pleasure riding, and driving. Work with horses is therapeutic to kids who come from troubled homes. When you care for a horse and work with a horse, it can you help you find yourself and make progress as a person.

There is so much diversity in the horse world today that it often seems as though there are a multitude of cliques to be a member of! My dear departed friend Ray Harmon once said, "I hate those cliques . . . unless, of course, I'm included in one!" But all these groups, whether they are from the city or the country, the desert or the mountains, are attracted to the noble creature, the horse. He can make you feel secure or insecure, safe or worried, confident or doubtful, cared about . . . or not! All depending on how the horse feels about you and how you work with him.

In this book you will enjoy quips and quotes from many people you've heard of and many you haven't. You may find yourself thinking, "I wish I'd said that!"

The wisdom, humor, and wit in these pages will entertain, and as you read, I bet you will hope, as I do, that the bond between people and horses will always be a part of the human condition.

—Buck Brannaman
July 2007

chapter one

We Turn to Horses: Some Opening Observations

Who would have thought that the horse, long ago replaced at its original jobs by machines, would return as one of the country's most important sport and recreational interests? . . . A century ago, people had horses in order to live; today many people live to have horses.
—ROBERT M. MILLER, D.V.M., AND RICK LAMB

• • •

Working with [horses] can be a very revealing time for the owner—any fear that was there to start with is greatly magnified. And I don't know anyone who wants the things below the surface of their psyches to be revealed publicly. Surprise! Around horses, it all comes to the surface.
—BUCK BRANNAMAN

• • •

A good horse has justice in his heart. I've seen it.
—CORMAC MCCARTHY

• • •

Despite our best efforts, horses and accidents are, unfortunately, related subjects. . . . According to one source, "[horseback] riding, motorcycling, and automobile racing are the three most dangerous sports."
—JAMES CLARK-DAWE, ESQ.

• • •

The extraordinary and thrilling affinity between the radically different minds of humans and horses has rewarded both humans and horses for thousands of years.
—SIMON BARNES

• • •

Nothing brings such innocent joy or such profound awareness that I am not invincible as the horseback experience.
—MELISSA SOVEY-NELSON, *IF I HAD A HORSE*

• • •

Of course horses can be wrong in their truthfulness—they may report a tiger in the laundry basket or a brace of dragons flying overhead—but this wrongness isn't deception. Horses do not lie.
—HELEN HUSHER, *CONVERSATIONS WITH A PRINCE*

• • •

My mom used to say, "Winnie Willis, in the beginning God created heaven and earth and horses. And sometimes I have to wonder if the good Lord shouldn't have quit while he was ahead."
—DANDI DALEY MACKALL

• • •

Like human beings, horses are all individuals with singular personalities, their own virtues and their own faults. We become bound to them for their beauty, their eccentricities, their heart and the love they so often return to us.
—LANA SLATON

• • •

The horse—the noblest, bravest, proudest, most courageous, and certainly the most perverse and infuriating animal that humans ever domesticated.
—ANNE MCCAFFREY

• • •

Think of the horse as a pure survivor. He's an animal other animals eat; therefore, by nature, he's afraid. This instinct has kept him alive for fifty million years.
—CRAIG CAMERON

• • •

[My mother] told me the better I behaved, the better I should be treated . . . "But," said she, "there are a great many kinds of men . . . I hope you will fall into good hands; but a horse never knows who may buy him, or who may drive him; it is all a chance for us."
—ANNA SEWELL, *BLACK BEAUTY: THE AUTOBIOGRAPHY OF A HORSE*

• • •

You cannot remain unmoved by the gentleness and conformation of a well-bred and well-trained horse—more than a thousand pounds of big-boned, well-muscled animal, slick coat and sweet of smell, obedient and mannerly, and yet forever a menace . . .
—ALBERT BORGMANN, *CROSSING THE POSTMODERN DIVIDE*

• • •

The grace and beauty of the horse enthralls us today in the same way it enthralled caveman artists if many millennia ago. Horses are living works of art.
—ROBERT M. MILLER, D.V.M., *UNDERSTANDING THE ANCIENT SECRETS OF THE HORSE'S MIND*

• • •

It is not the duty of the horse to be a biofeedback mechanism for yearning humans; yet it is remarkable how consistently people with horses claim to have learned much about themselves through them.
—TOM MCGUANE

• • •

You're not working on your horse, you're working on yourself.
—RAY HUNT

• • •

Even in the twenty-first century, we turn to horses. No, let me rephrase that. Especially in the twenty-first century, we turn to horses.
—SIMON BARNES

• • •

chapter two

Ages of the Horse: Horses through History

Once tamed, horses changed human history.
—PATRICIA LAUBER, *THE TRUE-OR-FALSE BOOK OF HORSES*

• • •

Horseshoes were common by the eleventh century, and by the twelfth century were being mass produced.
—DEBORAH EVE RUBIN, *HORSE TRIVIA: A HIPPOFILE'S DELIGHT*

• • •

In the late 1920s, man-versus-horse races became popular across the country. [In 1927] Paul "Hardrock" Simpson . . . took on a Texas pony named Maude in 500-mile race with a $500 prize. Exhausted, they both called it quits after two days. Simpson had covered 145 miles; Maude, 150.
—JOANNA SAYAGO, *RUNNER'S WORLD*

• • •

The horse was acquired by the Sioux in 1770. By 1890 we were all confined to reservations. We still had horses, but we were no longer the great horse culture living that life.
—LINDA LITTLE WOLF

• • •

They had metal sandals for the Roman draft horses that they tied on to the horse's foot with a thong, but those could go no faster than a walk, so they were not used for the cavalry horses.
—SABINE KELLS

• • •

The largest horse in history was a Shire horse named Sampson, later renamed Mammoth, foaled in 1846 in Bedfordshire, England. He stood 21.2$^{1/2}$ hands high (i.e., 7 ft. 2$^{1/2}$ in. or 2.20m), and his peak weight was estimated at over 3,300 pounds.
—WIKIPEDIA

• • •

The knowledge of how to care for horses went from common-place and normal to rare and esoteric in one generation. . . . The generation that preceded the First World War was raised in the Age of the Horse; the generation that followed was raised in the Age of the Automobile.
—MARGARET KORDA AND MICHAEL KORDA, *HORSE HOUSEKEEPING*

• • •

For at least fourteen thousand years before the arrival of the horse, Native Americans used dogs in everyday life. . . . When horses came along, it was only natural . . . to view them as big dogs. The horse was called big dog, medicine dog, elk dog, spirit dog, and mysterious dog.
—GAWANI PONY BOY

• • •

The Bedouin people customarily congratulated each other on three occasions: The birth of a son, the emergence of a poet within a tribe, and when a foal was born.
—BACHIR BSERANI

• • •

In backwoods justice, horse stealing was worse than manslaughter and a frequent occasion for lynching. To call a man a horse thief was the ultimate insult.
DEBORAH EVE RUBIN, *HORSE TRIVIA: A HIPPOFILE'S DELIGHT*

• • •

The difference between people who own horses and horsemen is that horsemen are people who appreciate the sacrifice a horse has made to have a relationship with a predator—a human being.
—E. W. "BUFF" HILDRETH

• • •

May you always ride a good horse!
—RICHARD SHRAKE

• • •

People who have never lived on horseback and are not familiar with the big pastures in rough country would not understand the feeling that is developed among all members of a ranch family for certain individual horses.
—BEN K. GREEN

• • •

A prince is never surrounded by as much majesty on his throne as he is on a beautiful horse.
—WILLIAM CAVENDISH (1592–1676)

• • •

Men on horseback have created most of the world's history.
—ANONYMOUS

• • •

Horses are humanity's best friends. They have done everything for us, their friends. Think about war. Think about bad weather. Think about the Wild West in America. What would they have done without the horse?
—GEORGE THEODORESCU

• • •

A horse is a safer bet than the trains.
—BORIS JOHNSON

• • •

I saw the World Spirit seated on a horse.
—GEORG WILHELM FRIEDRICH HEGEL (1770–1831)

• • •

The big horse market was the Army. You could get $200 for a gelding while a cow and a calf only sold for $40 to $50 and a new car for $1,000 so you could purchase a new car for five geldings. One day alone, I sold 185 horses to the army remount service.
—HARRY WIESCAMP

• • •

In London's fashionable West End, the mews—where tiny houses and apartments now sell for a fortune—were merely cobbled alleyways behind the great houses, where the family's horse (or horses) were kept, and above whose stable the coachman and the groom were lodged.
—MARGARET KORDA AND MICHAEL KORDA, *HORSE HOUSEKEEPING*

• • •

Remember that the most important gait of the hunter is the halt.
—WILLIAM P. WADSWORTH

• • •

The origin of the Arabian horse is a great zoological mystery. When we first encounter him, he is somewhat smaller than his counterpart today. Otherwise, he has remained unchanged through all the centuries. "As old as time itself and as fleet as its flying moments" perfectly describes him.
—JUDITH FORBIS, *THE CLASSIC ARABIAN HORSE*

• • •

The North African mule talks always of his mother's brother, the horse, but never of his father, the donkey, in favor of others supposedly more reputable.
—CLIFFORD GEERTZ

• • •

A good example of a simple technology with profound historical consequences is hay. Nobody knows who invented hay, the idea of cutting grass in the autumn and storing it in large enough quantities to keep horses and cows alive through the winter.
—FREEMAN DYSON, *INFINITE IN ALL DIRECTIONS*

• • •

The cowboys . . . each have to undergo much hard toil . . . on account of the extreme slowness with which everything must be done, as trail cattle should never be hurried.
—THEODORE ROOSEVELT (1858–1919)

• • •

Many a man who sticks constantly to the roads and lines of gates, who, from principle, never looks at a fence, is much attached to hunting. Some of those who have borne great names as Nimrods in our hunting annals would as life have led a forlorn hope as to put a horse in flight of hurdles.
—ANTHONY TROLLOPE

• • •

As long as wild horses are galloping free,
I'll dream of the West as I want it to be.
—RITA AND CHARLIE SUMMERS

• • •

It was quite customary as late as 1890 to see a countryman returning from the market, fast asleep, slumped forward over his saddle bar while his horse plodded his own way home.
—DOROTHY HARTLEY

• • •

Certainly the opening of the western frontiers of America was made possible by horses that were ridden and packed under saddle and those that worked in harness.
—ANDY RUSSELL, *HORSES AND HORSEMEN*

• • •

Traces of ancient horse manure have been found in a remote 5,600-year-old Kazakh village—a discovery that could be the earliest known evidence of horse domestication.
—NATIONALGEOGRAPHIC.COM

• • •

The history of horsemanship is less about sugar than pepper, less about light than dark, less about mindful kindness than thoughtless cruelty.
—LAWRENCE SCANLAN

• • •

Assault was content. Life was good here. It was probably even better for him, he thought, than it was for the mustang horses who used to run here wild and free nearly one hundred years ago.
—MARJORIE HODGSON PARKER

• • •

Though I am an old horse . . . I never yet could make out why men are so fond of this sport; they often hurt themselves, often spoil good horses, and tear up the fields, and all for a hare, or a fox, or a stag . . . but we are only horses, and don't know.
—ANNA SEWELL

• • •

I got a horse for my cowboy . . . best trade I ever made!
—ANONYMOUS

• • •

[I]f one squadron of horse cavalry . . . had been available to me at San Stefano . . . they would have enabled me to cut off and capture the entire German force opposing me along the north coast road and would have permitted my entry into Messina at least forty-eight hours earlier.
—LT. GEN. L. K. TRUSCOT JR., DURING WORLD WAR II

• • •

Cowboys call skill with horses being "handy."
—CHRIS IRWIN, *HORSES DON'T LIE*

• • •

In some ways American hunting in the early twentieth century, when it became officially organized with associations and "recognized hunts," was more English than the English, a way for nouveau riche northern plutocrats and faded-glory southern gentry to burnish their self-styled aristocratic images.
—STEPHEN BUDIANSKY, *TALLYHO AND TRIBULATION*

• • •

The equine influence reaches far back, to where the first captive horse was likely found in a bog by hunters somewhere in Europe or Asia.
—ANDY RUSSELL, *HORSES AND HORSEMEN*

• • •

Through our entire history we have become accustomed to pushing [animals] around in ways dictated by our own wants and needs without much regard for theirs.
—STANLEY SCHMIDT

• • •

Other times he could not afford to eat. But there was never a day when he wanted to trade his chaps for a job with a boss looking over his shoulder.
—DIRK JOHNSON, *A COWBOY'S LAST CHANCE*

• • •

The first Marchioness [of Salisbury] was painted by Sir Joshua Reynolds, and hunted till the day she died at eighty-five, when, half-blind and strapped to the saddle, she was accompanied by a groom who would shout, when her horse approached a fence, "Jump, dammit, my Lady, jump!"
—BARBARA TUCHMAN, *THE PROUD TOWER*

• • •

Of all the animals the horse is the best friend of the Indian, for without it he could not go on long journeys. A horse is the Indian's most valuable piece of property.
—BRAVE BUFFALO, A TETON SIOUX MEDICINE MAN

• • •

Western fieldwork conjures up images of struggle on horseback.
—STEPHEN JAY GOULD

• • •

Maybe early man, tired of wearing down his callused feet on hard trails, watched . . . a wild horse herd thunder by. . . . Covetous of the speed and freedom promised . . . he may have woven a rope . . . hung it on a limb over a trail leading to water and hid to wait.
—ANDY RUSSELL, *HORSES AND HORSEMEN*

• • •

About four o'clock in the afternoon . . . he turns up at the hunting stables . . . he says nothing of himself. . . . Why should he tell that he had been nearly an hour on foot trying to catch his horse, that he had sat himself down on a bank and almost cried, and that he had drained his flask . . . before one o'clock?
—ANTHONY TROLLOPE

• • •

In Westerns you were permitted to kiss your horse but never
your girl.
—GARY COOPER

• • •

The story is told of a man who, seeing one of the thoroughbred
stables for the first time, suddenly removed his hat and said in
awed tones, "My Lord! The cathedral of the horse."
—*KENTUCKY: A GUIDE TO THE BLUEGRASS STATE
(THE WPA GUIDE TO KENTUCKY)*

• • •

Fox hunting is essentially an inner struggle against dashed hopes.
It is an elemental experience for horse and human being alike.
—STEPHEN BUDIANSKY, *TALLYHO AND
TRIBULATION*

• • •

Of the horse I will say nothing because I know the times.
—LEONARDO DA VINCI (1452–1519), ON A HUGE
EQUESTRIAN STATUE THAT LEONARDO HAD BEEN
COMMISSIONED TO DESIGN AND CREATE, BUT
WHICH WAS NEVER CAST UNTIL MORE THAN FIVE
HUNDRED YEARS LATER, IN 1999, WHEN TWO HUGE
STATUES BASED UPON HIS DESIGN WERE FINALLY
MADE.

• • •

chapter three

ࡘ

Horse Power: Great Horses

Napoleon's famous horse Marengo, George Washington's gray
Arab Magnolia, Grant's horse Cincinnati, Lee's horse Traveller,
and Comanche, the one horse to survive the Battle of the Little
Big Horn, were regarded with awe because horses, even the bones
of horses, remember everything.
—TOM MCGUANE

• • •

Johnny Tivio, April 24, 1956, to April 24, 1981. Known to all as
the greatest all-around working horse ever to enter an arena.
—EPITAPH ON THE GRAVESTONE OF MONTY
ROBERTS'S JOHNNY TIVIO

• • •

Every so often, perhaps once every fifteen or twenty years, there comes to racing a horse so perfectly conformed, so talented and so tragic that it breaks the hearts of even the most hardened horsemen. Such a horse was the filly Ruffian.
—*THE COMPLETE BOOK OF THOROUGHBRED RACING*

• • •

Nothing focused the nation's mourning like the riderless black horse in the funeral cortege of John Kennedy.
—TOM MCGUANE, ON BLACK JACK, NAMED IN HONOR OF GENERAL JOHN J. "BLACK JACK" PERSHING

• • •

Nothing can take away the horror of seeing a horse break down. It's like seeing a masterpiece destroyed.
—JACK WHITAKER, ON THE TRAGIC 1975 MATCH RACE BETWEEN FOOLISH PLEASURE AND RUFFIAN

• • •

In 1938, near the end of a decade of monumental turmoil, the year's number-one newsmaker was not Franklin Delano Roosevelt, Hitler, or Mussolini. . . . The subject of the most newspaper column inches in 1938 wasn't even a person. It was an undersized, crooked-legged racehorse named Seabiscuit.
—LAURA HILLENBRAND, *SEABISCUIT: AN AMERICAN LEGEND*

• • •

It is a curious fact that today, two centuries later, the name of the Godolphin Arabian is found in the pedigree of almost every superior Thoroughbred. His blood reigns. To him goes the title: Father of the Turf.
—MARGUERITE HENRY, *KING OF THE WIND: THE STORY OF THE GODOLPHIN ARABIAN*

• • •

The Arabian stallion is magnificent, and the mare quite glamorous, but the airy-fairy foal is so delicate and fawn-like, he steals your heart away!
—GLADYS BROWN EDWARDS, *KNOW THE ARABIAN HORSE*

• • •

There are various ways to talk about what could possibly motivate a horse, or any animal, to such an effort. Fear certainly does not do it. Courage, joy, exaltation are more like it, but beyond that horses have, some of the time, a strong sense of artistry.
—VICKI HEARNE

• • •

No two paint horses are marked alike, so to own one is to own one of Mother Nature's original pieces of art.
—HARDY OELKE, *THE PAINT HORSE: AN AMERICAN TREASURE*

• • •

Silvery, shining, radiant, like something in a dream. Only she
wasn't a dream. She was real.
—JANE SCHWARTZ, *RUFFIAN: BURNING FROM THE
START*

• • •

I know great horses live again.
—STANLEY HARRISON

• • •

Dad said I looked and moved a lot like his great-grandfather, the
legendary Secretariat. My mom knew she had something special
. . . In fact, if other horses came near me, she would run at them
with ears pinned back and give them a swift kick. Now that could
smart!
—ROBERT L. MERZ

• • •

From 1936 to 1940, Seabiscuit endured a remarkable run of bad
fortune, conspiracy, and injury to establish himself as one of history's most extraordinary athletes. Graced with blistering speed,
tactical versatility, and indomitable will, he . . . shattered more
than a dozen track records.
—LAURA HILLENBRAND, *SEABISCUIT: AN AMERICAN
LEGEND*

• • •

There is a notion that you get only one great horse in a lifetime, a
persistent notion that I hope isn't true; because if that's the case,
I've already had mine.
—THOMAS MCGUANE

• • •

If I was an artist like you, I would draw a true picture of Traveller . . . But I am no artist and can therefore only say he is a Confederate grey.
—ROBERT E. LEE, IN A NOTE TO HIS WIFE'S COUSIN WHO WISHED TO PAINT A PORTRAIT OF LEE'S HORSE, TRAVELLER

• • •

I like Cutter because he has the fabled "eye of the eagle" . . . I just didn't know he could fly.
—GREG BRASS

• • •

I could see he felt entitled to a compliment, and so I said I had never seen lightning go like that horse. And I never had.
—MARK TWAIN

• • •

Some people show evil as a great racehorse shows breeding. They have the dignity of a hard chancre.
—ERNEST HEMINGWAY (1899–1961)

• • •

Wherever Domino's blood has gone, speed and courage have followed.
—AVALYN HUNTER, *THE KINGMAKER*

• • •

Somebody . . . has said that a fine man on a fine horse is the noblest bodily object in the world.
—G. K. CHESTERTON, *THE EVERLASTING MAN*

• • •

"Speed Miracle"
—THE *NEW YORK TIMES*, ON MAN O' WAR AFTER
SETTING ASTONISHING SPEED RECORDS

• • •

On the bright cold afternoon of November 12, 1973 . . . several
hundred people gathered at Blue Grass Airport in Lexington to
greet Secretariat after his flight from New York into retirement in
Kentucky.
—WILLIAM NACK

• • •

In the course of his sixteen-month racing career, Secretariat
rose higher and faster and larger than any U.S. horse of modern
times.
—WILLIAM NACK

• • •

Even his name was un-regal. Funny Cide. It sounded like
laughing yourself to death.
—SALLY JENKINS, *FUNNY CIDE*

• • •

Man o' War suffered his only defeat in the 1919 Sanford Stakes
to a horse named Upset.
—BILL HELLER

• • •

Here lies the fleetest runner the American Turf has ever known,
and one of the gamest and most generous of horses.
—INSCRIPTION ON THE GRAVE OF DOMINO

• • •

In the darkest days of depression and war, a horse named Seabiscuit elevated our country's spirit and embodied the qualities we cherish in our horses; heart, drive, loyalty, love, and playfulness.
—*CHICKEN SOUP FOR THE HORSE LOVER'S SOUL*

• • •

"You wanna see the best-lookin' two-year-old you've ever seen? . . . What do you think? . . . Don't forget the name: Secretariat. He can run. . . . Don't quote me, but this horse will make them all forget Riva Ridge."
—JIMMY GAFFNEY

• • •

His greatest performance was almost certainly his match race with the 1894 Belmont Stakes winner Henry of Navarre; over a distance of nine furlongs, at least an eighth of a mile farther than he cared to go, Domino absolutely refused to be defeated and ran Henry to a dead heat.
—AVALYN HUNTER, *THE KINGMAKER*

• • •

Magnanimous in defeat, he was a superb loser and did not waste time dwelling on what might have been.
—VINCENT O'BRIEN, ON SANGSTER

• • •

I'm a red, chestnut colt of average size. They say my best features are a fine head and lustrous red coat. I've been nicknamed "Little Red" after my ancestor Secretariat who of course was "Big Red." Although not a big horse, I have been referred to by my trainers as "A little piece of iron."
—ROBERT L. MERZ

• • •

"There's more people out here to meet Secretariat than there was to greet the governor." "Well, he's won more races than the governor," pilot Dan Neff replied.
—WILLIAM NACK

• • •

De mostest hoss that ever wuz.
—WILL HARBUT, EULOGIZING MAN O' WAR

• • •

In more than three hundred years of New York racing, no filly or mare had ever lugged such a load on the flat. In a sense the voters were right. She isn't Horse of the Year. She's the Horse of Three Centuries.
—RED SMITH

• • •

Barbaro was euthanized Monday after complications from his gruesome breakdown at last year's Preakness, ending an eight-month ordeal that made him even more of a hero than he was as a champion on the track.
—ANONYMOUS

• • •

Based on looks and lineage, Seattle Slew at birth could not have been termed a horse destined for greatness. "He was ugly. . . . He had big ears, and they flopped all over the first week."
—DAN MEARNS

• • •

Here is living harmony in horseflesh; an embodiment of rhythm and modulation, of point and counterpoint, that sang to the eye and made music in the heart.
—JOHN HERVEY, ON EQUIPOISE

• • •

His trainer said that managing him was like holding a tiger by the tail. His owner compared him to "chain lightning." His jockeys found their lives transformed by him, in triumphant . . . ways.
—DOROTHY OURS, *MAN O' WAR: A LEGEND LIKE LIGHTNING*

• • •

A fine horse or a beautiful woman, I cannot look at them unmoved, even now when seventy winters have chilled my blood.
—SIR ARTHUR CONAN DOYLE

• • •

I am very pleased with Smarty's move. I wanted him to finish up strong, and he did.
—JOHN SERVIS, SMARTY JONES'S TRAINER

• • •

As a physical specimen, Secretariat had a muscular build that belied his youth. As an athlete, he moved with breathtaking style, combining the raw power of a fullback with the agility of an Olympic gymnast.
—*THE 10 BEST KENTUCKY DERBIES*

• • •

"If man breeds one genius to a decade it is enough. And so it goes with hawses . . . In those days ninety colts were foaled each spring at Sanfo'd Hall. . . . How many hawses—truly great hawses—did such brood mayehs as that produce? How many do you think?"
"Not many, " he murmured.
—JOHN TAINTOR FOOTE

• • •

Most racehorses that amount to anything, which is to say they win stakes races, have pedigrees that on hindsight have a stakes winning tinge. The adage that all racehorses are well-bred of one goes far back enough is one of the glorious ironies of a tradition-rich sport.
—TIMOTHY T. CAPPS, *SPECTACULAR BID*

• • •

[He] was blessed to have forgotten his binoculars.
—TOM CALLAHAN, ON CHARLIE WHITTINGHAM WHEN HIS HORSE FERDINAND WON THE KENTUCKY DERBY

• • •

I was born with the perfect combination of athleticism and power. I weigh a little more than a half ton and can reach speeds of up to 45 miles per hour. I wear what are known as racing plates, or as you call them, horseshoes. . . . I want all the sneaker companies to know I'm available as a spokeshorse.
—ROBERT L. MERZ

• • •

Once he strengthened up, you could do whatever you wanted on him. It was like driving a Ferrari rather than a Cortina.
—COLIN BROWN, FORMER JOCKEY ON DESERT ORCHID

• • •

Ask anyone on the street for one name in horse racing and they will always say Secretariat. He is the definitive touchstone between racing and the American public.
—PENNY CHENERY, OWNER OF SECRETARIAT

• • •

My father hated selling horses, he was afraid the good one was going to get away.
—ROBERT LEHMAN,

• • •

Funny Cide wasn't the product of money and breeding, but rather, of the vast middle class in horse racing. Had he belonged to a larger stable, or fallen into the hands of a less conscientious trainer, he might not have become what he did. But he was a fortunate horse.
—SALLY JENKINS, *FUNNY CIDE*

• • •

She stumbled coming out of the gate, and that will be part of the legacy of Rags to Riches—the sudden stabbing fear of danger. [. . .] But she regained her equilibrium quickly and caught up with the colts, and now racing has a new champion, a new story, a new hope.
—GEORGE VECSEY ON RAGS TO RICHES, WHO IN 2007 BECAME ONLY THE THIRD FILLY TO WIN THE 139-YEAR-OLD BELMONT STAKES, AND THE FIRST TO DO SO SINCE 1905

• • •

"We just invested in a dream. . . . We didn't take a chance on Funny Cide . . . he took a chance on us. This little horse has helped us show the world that sometimes the dreams of the little guy *do* come true. . . . Funny Cide rewarded us all in far greater ways than we ever deserved."
—CHRIS RUSSELL-GRABB, *THE FUNNY CIDE OF LIFE*

• • •

On the turn I could see all the horses clearly at once, but the image I remember is that of the reddish brown colt going by three horses so fast it made me blink. Twice he changed gears to avoid further trouble. . . . "A freak," I said to myself.
—STEVE DAVIDOWITZ, *BETTING THOROUGBREDS*

• • •

He's good enough for me. I won't say he's a superhorse because you're never a superhorse until you're retired. Any horse can be beaten on any given day.
—ANGEL CORDERO JR.

• • •

"The Biscuit [Seabiscuit], he'd lay back and let them come right up, side-to-side, get them feeling like the match was theirs, then he'd look them in the eye and take off like a bullet." Floss laughed out loud at that.
—THERESA PELUSO, *AN UNLIKELY TRIO OF HOPE*

• • •

Man o' War . . . won twenty of his twenty-one races. . . . "Big Red," as he was known, lived to be thirty and became a symbol of American force and durability, so beloved that his birthday party was once broadcast to the nation on NBC Radio.
—ERIC RACHLIS, BLOSSOM LEFCOURT, AND BERT MORGAN, *HORSE RACING: THE GOLDEN AGE OF THE TRACK*

• • •

And it was not Foolish Pleasure whose importance—whose symbolic importance—had transcended the world of racing and even sports in general. It was the larger-than-life filly with the perfect record; the coal black daughter of Reviewer and Shenanigans; the speedball, the beauty, the female, the freak.
—JANE SCHWARTZ

• • •

On the long ride from Louisville, I would regale them with stories about the horse [Secretariat]. . . . Oh, I knew all the stories, knew them well. . . . Knew them as I knew the stories of my children. Knew them as I knew stories of my own life.
—WILLIAM NACK

• • •

Even the most forlorn thoroughbred, seen at a distance—like a woman outside the fence at an army camp—is flawlessly beautiful.
—JOE FLAHERTY

• • •

I really liked Lassie, but that horse, Flicka, was a nasty animal with a terrible disposition. All the Flickas—all six of them—were awful.
—RODDY MCDOWALL

• • •

He's a proper horse. He's brilliant.
—RUBY WALSH, ON HEDGEHUNTER

• • •

Once trainer Louis Feustel unleashed Man o' War onto the . . .
sports scene, the colt was quick about the business of ensuring
that he would rank with such athletes as Babe Ruth, Jack
Dempsey, and Red Grange among the hallowed sports figures
produced by his era.
—THE BLOOD-HORSE STAFF, *THOROUGHBRED
CHAMPIONS*

• • •

The average colt has a stride of 24.6 feet, according to Equix,
a company in Lexington, Kentucky, that conducts biometrical
analyses of Thoroughbreds. Secretariat's was 24.8. Bernardini,
in the Preakness, checked in at 26.5 feet—"off the charts," says
Ginger Sanders, Equix's president
—TOMMY CRAGGS

• • •

A champion racehorse at the winning line, unattached, eats the
blooms of his victory wreath.
—SAIOM SHRIVER

• • •

All our best horses have Arab blood, and once in a while it seems
to have come out strong and show in every part of the creature,
in his frame, his power, and his wild, free, roving spirit.
—ERNEST THOMPSON SETON

• • •

On rare occasions, a horse like Funny Cide . . . comes along . . . reminding people just how much a racehorse and this sport can affect a person, a town, a city, a state, a country.
—STEVE HAKSIN

• • •

[O]nly ten colts have won the Triple Crown since Sir Barton first did it in 1919 . . . a dynasty of equine royalty as distinguished as the aristocratic families.
—ERIC RACHLIS, BLOSSOM LEFCOURT, AND BERT MORGAN, *HORSE RACING: THE GOLDEN AGE OF THE TRACK*

• • •

Secretariat is blazing along! The first three-quarters of a mile in 1:09 . . . Secretariat is widening now. He is moving like a tremendous machine!
—ANNOUNCER CHIC ANDERSON, AT THE BELMONT STAKES IN 1973

• • •

A racehorse that consistently runs just a second faster than another horse is worth millions of dollars more. Be willing to give that extra effort that separates the winner from the one in second place.
—H. JACKSON BROWN JR.

• • •

Twenty-nine lengths. Thirty. The colt took a final leap. Thirty-one. The timer froze: 2:24 . . . it is frozen there still.
—WILLIAM NACK

• • •

He was as near living flame as horses ever get.
—JOE PALMER, ON MAN O' WAR

• • •

I am still under the impression that there is nothing alive quite so beautiful as a Thoroughbred horse.
—JOHN GALSWORTHY

• • •

Black Ruby knows exactly where the finish line is, and she just refuses to lose . . . She always seems to find that extra gear, call it "mulepower" if you will.
—DEBRA GINSBURG, *THE FASTEST MULE IN THE WEST*

• • •

He was a man of few words, but he had something to say to me that morning. He said, 'Son, there is no way you can get this horse beat today . . . Believe me, boy, you are riding the greatest horse of all time and I have seen them all.'
—RON TURCOTTE, SECRETARIAT'S JOCKEY, RECALLING WHAT HOLLIE HUGHES TOLD HIM BEFORE THE 1973 BELMONT STAKES

• • •

If this isn't a Triple Crown horse, I don't know what one looks like.
—BARCLAY TAGG, ON A HORSE NAMED NOBIZ LIKE SHOBIZ

• • •

The ultimate equipment change.
—D. WAYNE LUKAS, ON FUNNY CIDE

• • •

[E]leven victories in eleven starts. The highlights included the
Belmont Stakes by twenty lengths; the Dwyer over the audacious
effort by John P. Grier to bring him to a drive in the stretch; the
Lawrence Realization by a recorded one hundred lengths.
—THE BLOOD-HORSE STAFF, *THOROUGHBRED
CHAMPIONS*

• • •

Arabians: A little bit of everything perfect.
—AMANDA FERBER

• • •

I used to think the greatest thing I ever saw was the Ali-Frazier fight in Madison Square Garden. This was even better.
—PETE AXTHELM, ON SECRETARIAT'S THIRTY-ONE-LENGTH VICTORY IN THE BELMONT STAKES

• • •

His [Funny Cide] run in the Preakness left everyone but the horses breathless, winning by an astounding nine and three-quarter lengths.
—CHRIS RUSSELL-GRABB, *THE FUNNY CIDE OF LIFE*

• • •

Horses have a way of getting inside you, and so it was that Secretariat became like a fifth child in our house.
—WILLIAM NACK

• • •

His nature just speaks to me. I didn't want him too far back to get dirt in his face, to get discouraged.
—JULIE KRONE, ON COLONIAL AFFAIR

• • •

[Thoroughbreds] are exuberant. They are sensitive. They have opinions. They in general have too much of every lively quality than too little.
—JANE SMILEY

• • •

Winner of twenty races in twenty-one starts, Man o' War had earned a record at the time, $249,465.
—THE BLOOD-HORSE STAFF, *THOROUGHBRED CHAMPIONS*

• • •

The most important thing I learned from Johnny . . . was that when he had been abused and forced, he didn't reach his full potential. When there was a request rather than demand, and love instead of neglect, he was able to perform like no other horse before him.
—MONTY ROBERTS

• • •

Secretariat became the most expensive animal in history when he was sold to a breeding syndicate for the then shocking sum of $6.08 million.
—WILLIAM NACK

• • •

Other than being castrated, things have gone quite well for Funny Cide.
—KENNY MAYNE, BEFORE THE RUNNING OF THE BELMONT STAKES

• • •

chapter four

Horselaughs: The Humorous Horse

Most of our horses . . . are . . . named from some feat or pecu-
liarity. Wire Fence . . . ran into one of the abominations after
which he is now called. . . . Fall Back would never get to the front.
. . . Water Skip always jumps mud puddles; and there are dozens
others with names as purely descriptive.
—THEODORE ROOSEVELT

• • •

Feed 'em and lead 'em.
—CONFORMATION CLASSES IN A NUTSHELL

• • •

I watched a rerun on television of a 1960s comedy program called *Mr. Ed*, which was about a talking horse. Judging by the quality of the jokes, I would guess that Mr. Ed wrote his own material.
—BILL BRYSON, *THE LOST CONTINENT: TRAVELS IN SMALL-TOWN AMERICA*

• • •

If you can lead it to water and force it to drink, it isn't a horse.
—ANONYMOUS

• • •

Gordon Wright was showing a jumper at the National Horse Show. He had just had one of his books published, and when his horse stopped at a fence, Joe Green, who has a voice that could carry, yelled in from the in gate, "Hey, Gordon, what chapter is that in?!"
—CLARENCE "HONEY" CRAVEN

• • •

And do you think Paul Revere even would have looked at a horse if all the taxis hadn't been engaged with the theater crowds that night?
—RING LARDNER, *TIPS ON HORSES*

• • •

A horse is not only good fun, it is also a beautiful-looking psychotherapist who lives on grass and doesn't charge by the hour!
—PERRY WOOD

• • •

In England I would rather be a man, a horse, a dog, or a woman, in that order. In America I think the order would be reversed.
—BRUCE GOULD

• • •

Honey Rider beat Film Maker by a nose for the win. Or as track announcer Durkin called it, "Honey Rider . . . by a nostril!"
—C. N. Richardson, *Remembering Forego—The Handicap Horse of The Decade*

• • •

When will they make a tractor that can furnish the manure for farm fields and produce a baby tractor every spring?
—GEORGE RUPP

• • •

Yesterday I moved a ton of manure. Actually, it was the horses who moved it; I merely pitched it into a wheelbarrow.
—MELISSA PIERSON

• • •

Horse sense is the thing a horse has which keeps it from betting on people.
—W. C. FIELDS (1880–1946)

• • •

Be wary of the horse with a sense of humor.
—PAM BROWN

• • •

When you're young and you fall off a horse, you may break something. When you're my age and you fall off, you splatter.
—ROY ROGERS

• • •

He knows when you are happy. He knows when you are proud. He also knows when you have a carrot.
—ANONYMOUS

• • •

You're better off betting on a horse than betting on a man. A horse may not be able to hold you tight, but he doesn't wanna wander from the stable at night.
—BETTY GRABLE (1916–1973)

• • •

Whoever said a horse was dumb, was dumb.
—WILL ROGERS

• • •

Found a smoldering cigarette left by a horse.
—DAVE BARRY

• • •

It's a lot like nuts and bolts—if the rider's nuts, the horse bolts!
—NICHOLAS EVANS

• • •

Whenever you observe a horse closely, you feel as if a human being sitting inside were making fun of you.
—ELIAS CANETTI

• • •

Defenders of le Horse will . . . point to the term "good, common horse sense," . . . as being proof of the beast's virtues, but if a horse has such good common sense, why do they always have to have a jockey show them the way round a . . . race track when you couldn't possibly go wrong unlest you was dumb.
—RING LARDNER, *TIPS ON HORSES*

• • •

The horse bit the pastor. How came this to pass? He heard the good pastor say, "All flesh is grass."
—EMMET GRIBBIN JR., IN A LETTER TO *LIVING CHURCH* MAGAZINE

• • •

All I pay my psychiatrist is the cost of feed and hay, and he'll listen to me any day.
—ANONYMOUS

• • •

If the world was truly a rational place, men would ride side-saddle.
—RITA MAE BROWN

• • •

The mule was asked: "Who is your father?" It responded with: "The horse is my uncle."
—ARABIC PROVERB

• • •

I never play horseshoes 'cause Mother taught us not to throw our clothes around.
—MR. ED, THE TALKING HORSE OF THE 1960S TV SERIES

• • •

Even an E-type Jaguar looks merely flash beside a really smart pony and trap.
—MARION C. GARRETTY

• • •

How do you catch a loose horse? Make a noise like a carrot.
—BRITISH CAVALRY JOKE

• • •

I've fallen in love with my horse. It's a safer bet. We all know from my illustrious past that I should be sticking to men with four legs.
—SHARON STONE

• • •

We are . . . a small army composed of slave masters who are in turn enslaved by our slaves. We are the ones who assiduously pick up their excrement . . . We bathe, curry, brush, mane-pull, tail-detangle, hoof-pick and take off and put on blankets . . . They stand there and loudly demand their food.
—MELISSA PIERSON

• • •

Few girls are as well-shaped as a good horse.
—HANNAH ARENDT

• • •

In horse vernacular, Roy has always "given me my head," and I
have tried to do the same for him.
—DALE EVANS

• • •

You know horses are smarter than people. You never heard of a
horse going broke betting on people.
—WILL ROGERS

• • •

The Budweiser Clydesdales! I'm so glad to see you. Now that
John Wayne and Elvis are gone, you're all we have left!
—CB MESSAGE FROM A DRIVER WHO SAW THE VANS
PULLING THE BUDWEISER CLYDESDALES

• • •

There has to be a woman, but not much of a one. A good horse is
much more important.
—MAX BRAND (1892–1944), ON WRITING WESTERNS

• • •

Hundreds and hundreds of beautiful horses in the [Santa Bar-
bara] parade, and a man without a silver saddle is a vagrant.
—WILL ROGERS

• • •

When any one of our relations was found to be a person of a very bad character . . . or one we desired to get rid of, upon his leaving my house I . . . lend him a riding-coat, or a pair of boots, or sometimes a horse of small value, and I always had the satisfaction of finding he never came back to return them.
—OLIVER GOLDSMITH

• • •

"Your wife is extremely pretty . . . Does she ride?"
"I'm glad you like her looks," I replied, "as I fear you will find her thoroughly despicable otherwise. For one thing, she not only can't ride, but she believes that I can!"
—SOMERVILLE AND ROSS

• • •

"Later on, can I see Volponi?"
"Yeah, but . . . don't try to pet him, unless you want to start typing with your toes."
—JOE MCGINNISS, *THE BIG HORSE*

• • •

In my opinion, a horse is the animal to have. Eleven-hundred pounds of raw muscle, power, grace, and sweat between your legs—it's something you just can't get from a pet hamster.
—ANONYMOUS

• • •

On horseback he seemed to require as many hands as a Hindu god, at least four for clutching the reins, and two more for patting the horse soothingly on the neck.
—SAKI (H. H. MUNRO) (1870–1916)

• • •

They use the snaffle and the curb all right; But where's the bloody horse?
—ROY CAMPBELL

• • •

One of the earliest religious disappointments in a young girl's life devolves upon her unanswered prayer for a horse.
—PHILLIS THEROUX

• • •

A woman needs two animals—the horse of her dreams and a jackass to pay for it.
—ANONYMOUS

• • •

I prefer a bike to a horse. The brakes are more easily checked.
—LAMBERT JEFFRIES

• • •

Men are generally more careful of the Breed of their Horses and Dogs than of their Children.
—WILLIAM PENN (1644–1718)

• • •

The wildest broncos are those you rode some place else.
—KEN ALSTAD

• • •

You can lead a horse to water, and if you can train it to float on its back, you've got something.
—JOHNNY CARSON

• • •

You know you're a Horse Mom when: The equine feed bill is a bigger portion of your family budget than the human feed bill . . . ditto the medical bills . . . and shoes.
—BARBARA GREENSTREET, *ARE YOU A REAL HORSE MOM?*

• • •

Three things are men most likely to be cheated in, a horse, a wig, and a wife.
—BENJAMIN FRANKLIN (1706–1790)

• • •

I preferred a safe horse to a fast one—I would like to have an excessively gentle horse—a horse with no spirit whatever—a lame one, if he had such a thing. Inside of five minutes I was mounted, and perfectly satisfied with my outfit.
—MARK TWAIN

• • •

Computers are like horses—press the right button and they'll take you anywhere.
—ANONYMOUS

• • •

For the man . . . whose duty it is to sweep up manure, the supreme terror is the possibility of a world without horses. To tell him that it is disgusting to spend one's life shoveling up hot turds is a piece of imbecility. A man can get to love shit if his livelihood depends on it, if his happiness is involved.
—HENRY MILLER (1891–1980)

• • •

Changing horses in the middle of a stream, gets you wet and sometimes cold. . . . Changing faces in the middle of a dream gets you old . . . oh, gets you old.
—DAN FOGELBERG

• • •

Your horse has a reason to be vain. You don't.
—ANDREW GLASS

• • •

Proper scientific name for horses: Equus keepus brokeus.
—ANONYMOUS

• • •

The grass is green where the horse has pooped.
—ANNAMARIA TADLOCK

• • •

[Robert Frost] was like a horse you could get along with if you came up beside him on the okay side.
—ARCHIBALD MACLEISCH

• • •

Why, I'd horse-whip you if I had a horse.
—GROUCHO MARX

• • •

He was so learned that he could name a horse in nine languages; so ignorant that he bought a cow to ride on.
—BENJAMIN FRANKLIN

• • •

For some young women, horses become a substitute for boys,
who appear to be too much of a risk.
—GAWANI PONY BOY

• • •

Ticket seller: "Wait a minute . . . your ass just sneezed. And
horses can't talk. No, no . . . nothing here adds up at all."
—*FAMILY GUY*, FROM A SCENE IN WHICH BRIAN AND
CHRIS TRY TO SNEAK INTO A FAIR BY WEARING A
HORSE SUIT

• • •

Fight smog, buy a horse.
—CHARLOTTE MOORE

• • •

Electronic transfer of funds.
—WALTER T. KEES, WHEN ASKED FOR THE BEST
THING EVER SAID ABOUT HORSES

• • •

Whisky for my men, beer for my horses.
—WILLIE NELSON AND TOBY KEITH

• • •

Trust in God, but tie your horse.
—ANONYMOUS

• • •

I went to horseback riding camp. That's where I discovered Mötley Crüe and acid. My horse fantasies are combined with Mötley Crüe and hallucinogenics.
—MELISSA AUF DER MAUR

• • •

Keep away from women and horses and . . . If you love horses you'll get horse-shit.
—ERNEST HEMINGWAY

• • •

There are no handles to a horse, but the 1910 model has a string to each side of its face for turning its head when there is something you want it to see.
—STEPHEN LEACOCK (1869–1944)

• • •

In what other sport do you put on leather boots, stretch-fabric breeches, a shirt and tie, a wool jacket, a velvet-covered cap, and leather gloves, and then go out and exercise?
—A. LONDON WOLF, ON HORSE-SHOWING IN NINETY-DEGREE WEATHER

• • •

Women, I never met one yet that was half as reliable as a horse.
—JOHN WAYNE IN *NORTH TO ALASKA*

• • •

Why is it that a woman will ignore homicidal tendencies in a horse, but will be furious at a man for leaving a toilet seat up?
—ANONYMOUS

• • •

He's definitely one of those horses that walks the fine line
between genius and insanity.
—SUE BLINKS

• • •

"You know, Doctor," said the horse, "that vet over the hill knows
nothing at all. He has been treating me six weeks now—for
spavins. What I need is spectacles. I am going blind in one eye.
There's no reason why horses shouldn't wear glasses, the same as
people."
—HUGH LOFTING, *DOCTOR DOLITTLE*

• • •

You know you're a horse lover when you always keep carrots,
apples, and sugar cubes in your refrigerator.
—*CHICKEN SOUP FOR THE HORSE LOVER'S SOUL*

• • •

You know you're a horse lover when your favorite outfit is made
of leather and includes whips and spurs.
—*CHICKEN SOUP FOR THE HORSE LOVER'S SOUL*

• • •

I ride horses because it's the only sport where I can exercise while
sitting down.
—JOAN HANSEN

• • •

A horse that can count to ten is a remarkable horse, not a
remarkable mathematician.
—SAMUEL JOHNSON

• • •

chapter five

"My Kingdom for a Horse!": The Horse in Literature

With hearts pounding and breath quickening, the men . . . stared toward the silvered hills. Not four hundred yards away, they saw him coming! Fury—the ebony king of the range! He was moving at an easy gallop, his hoofs making hollow, drumlike sounds on the grass.

—ALBERT G. MILLER, *FURY: STALLION OF BROKEN WHEEL RANCH*

• • •

His son, Emile, had tried this foolish experiment of raising horses on the reef, and given his life under the stallion's hoofs.
—CHARLES TENNEY JACKSON, *THE HORSE OF HURRICANE REEF*

• • •

February's early morning chill filled the barn and steam billowed from the horse's heaving body and flared nostrils.
—EUGENE DAVIS, *FROM THE HORSE'S MOUTH*

• • •

Billy explained how to use a stick of licorice for a bit until Galiban was used to having something in his mouth. Billy explained, "Of course we could force-break him to everything, but he wouldn't be as good a horse if we did.
—JOHN STEINBECK (1902–1968)

• • •

In the pasture of dead horses, roots of pine trees pushed through the pale curves of your ribs, yellow blossoms flourished above you in autumn, and in winter frost heaved your bones in the ground—old toilers, soil makers; O Roger, Mackerel, Riley, Ned, Nellie, Chester, Lady Ghost.
—DONALD HALL, *NAMES OF HORSES*

• • •

I went up to the table, snatched up a glass of brandy and filled my mouth with it, then went back to the pony, took him by the head, and sent a squirt of brandy up each nostril; I squirted the rest down his throat.
—SOMERVILLE AND ROSS, *THE BAGMAN'S PONY*

• • •

"Are horses smart or dumb?" I asked Buster.
"They are very smart," he said with conviction. "Very intelligent.
And if you ask one to do something he was going to do anyway,
you hurt his feelings, you insult his intelligence."
—THOMAS MCGUANE, *BUSTER*

• • •

Thou shall be for Man a source of happiness and wealth; thy
back shall be a seat of honor, and thy belly of riches; every grain
of barley given thee shall purchase indulgence for the sinner.
—THE KORAN

• • •

At its best, the poetry of the open range remains, not in the
sacred, melodramatic antics of the stunt horses but in the preci-
sion of that minority singled out as "cow horses," sometimes lost
in the artificial atmosphere of the big events.
—THOMAS MCGUANE

• • •

No horse . . . can be courageous if it has no spirit.
—PLATO

• • •

He began to speak softly to the old horse but his voice was
steady, almost conversational, as though he was chatting to a
friend.
—JAMES HERRIOT, *ALL THINGS BRIGHT AND
BEAUTIFUL*

• • •

Give a man a horse he can ride,
Give a man a boat he can sail;
And his rank and wealth,
his strength and health on sea nor shore shall fail.
—JAMES THOMSON (1700–1748)

• • •

"Get up!" he shouted . . . And the great horse did so. First
plunging up, but with his haunches squatted in the water . . .
Then to all fours and standing and standing with his tail whipped
about on his heaving flanks. He seemed watching that wall of
blow water for the Gulf.
—CHARLES TENNEY JACKSON, *THE HORSE OF
HURRICANE REEF*

• • •

Stronger than that was sense of partnership between these
officers and their charges, the incredible bond between them
created by so many shared experiences and so many hours spent
together.
—TAD COFFIN

• • •

Man, encompassed by the elements which conspired to destroy
him, would have been a slave had not the horse made him a king.
—ANONYMOUS

• • •

The horses swam ashore to the same mysterious island—
Assateague—and for years afterward were seen by visitors from
the nearby mainland wandering the pine forests like shadows.
—RICH POMERANTZ, *WILD HORSES OF THE DUNES*

• • •

Far back, far back in our dark soul the horse prances . . . The
horse, the horse! The symbol of surging potency and power of
movement.
—D. H. LAWRENCE (1885–1930)

• • •

As I was going by Charing Cross,
I saw a black man upon a black horse.
They told me it was King Charles the First.
Oh dear, my heart was ready to burst!
—ANONYMOUS

• • •

"Many's the thousand miles I've walked after you, awd lad, and
many's the talk we've had together. But I didn't have to say much
to tha, did I? I reckon you knew every more I made, everything I
said. Just one little word and you always did what ah wanted you
to do."
—JAMES HERRIOT, *ALL THINGS BRIGHT AND
BEAUTIFUL*

• • •

She pulled his right ear, stroked it; then pressed her fingers against his poll. Duke's head came lower over her shoulder. His big lips twitched. He reached even lower and with his lips cleanly plucked a carrot from Pauline's jacket pocket.
—JOCELYN REEKIE, *THE WEEK OF THE HORSE*

• • •

She knew that the horse, born to serve nobly, had waited in vain for someone noble to serve. His spirit knew that nobility had gone out of men.
—D. H. LAWRENCE

• • •

Horse, thou art truly a creature without equal, for thou fliest without wings and conquerest without sword
—THE KORAN

• • •

Children, dogs, and horses is regarded in this country as sacred items and it is considered pretty close to a felony to even make a face when any of the three is mentioned.
—RING LARDNER, *TIPS ON HORSES*

• • •

Look at the horse . . . that great animal that stands so close to man.
—FYODOR DOSTOEVSKY (1821–1881)

• • •

"Well, this horse, he's eager, he's willing. He's straightforward and honest, you know. You ask him something and he understands. He's willing to work with you."
—GENE SMITH, *THE CHAMPION*

• • •

And God took a handful of southerly wind, blew His breath over it and created the horse.
—BEDOUIN SAYING

• • •

He outran the colts his own age and the seasoned running horses as well. He seemed not to know that he was an earthly creature with four legs, like other horses. He acted as if he were an airy thing, traveling on the wings of the wind.
—MARGUERITE HENRY, *KING OF THE WIND: THE STORY OF THE GODOLPHIN ARABIAN*

• • •

VILLAIN, A HORSE—
Villain, I say, give me a horse to fly,
To swim the river, villain, and to fly.
—GEORGE PEELE (1556–1596)

• • •

I turned away. I had dreamed great dreams. They were gone. There would never be another racehorse born in our barn.
—GENE SMITH, *THE CHAMPION*

• • •

He met her and fell in love and married her, and part of the wedding vows were "love me, love my horses." It was part and parcel of the whole relationship.
—COOKY MCCLUNG, *FROM SAILBOATS TO SNAFFLES IN ONE EASY MARRIAGE*

• • •

Suffering for the pleasure of others is nothing new to me. I have even begun to find a certain equine pleasure in it. Let him swagger, poor fellow! . . . thought the gelding, and stepping carefully on his crooked legs he went along the middle of the road.
—LEO TOLSTOY, *STRIDER—THE STORY OF A HORSE*

• • •

[T]he Lord looked down on a Sunday morning and saw that something was missing—something that represented His patience, His understanding, His love, His everything, indeed all that was good—and He created the horse.
—FRANZ MAIRINGER, *HORSES ARE MADE TO BE HORSES*

• • •

She could hardly wait for it to be morning. She was going to spend two whole weeks on a real farm with horses. What a perfect vacation!
—GERTRUDE CHANDLER WARNER

• • •

It was a great treat to us to be turned out into the home paddock or the old orchard. The grass was so cool and soft to our feet, the air so sweet, and the freedom to do as we liked was so pleasant— to gallop, to lie down, and roll over on our backs, or to nibble the sweet grass.
—ANNA SEWELL, *BLACK BEAUTY: THE AUTOBIOGRAPHY OF A HORSE*

• • •

The mares are for whoever is man enough to take them.
—CHARLES TENNEY JACKSON, *THE HORSE OF HURRICANE REEF*

• • •

[The horse] seemed hearkening with an exile's doubt to the new sounds of this new universe, testing the wide nostrils the taint in the wind of equine strangers, and studying with his eyes . . . far horizons.
—WILBUR DANIEL STEELE, *BLUE MURDER*

• • •

Yet when books have been read and reread, it boils down to the horse, his human companion, and what goes on between them.
—WALTER FARLEY

• • •

Every single movement of Florian's revealed nobility, grace, significance, and distinction all in one; and in each of his poses he was the ideal model for a sculptor, the composite of all the equestrian statues in history.
—FELIX SALTEN (1869–1945)

• • •

He is white and clearly one of the most beautiful horses I have ever beheld. Seeing him reminds one that there is still a God, even though we are in the middle of some dismal war.
—ANN RINALDI, *A RIDE INTO MORNING: THE STORY OF TEMPE WICK*

• • •

The great majority of men, especially in France, both desire and possess a fashionable woman, much in the way one might own a fine horse—as a luxury befitting a young man.
—HENRI B. STENDHAL

• • •

Higher and higher receded the sky, wider and wider spread the streak of dawn . . . People began to get up, and in the owner's stable-yard the sounds of snorting, the rustling of litter, and even the shrill angry neighing of horses crowded together and at variance about something, grew more and more frequent
—LEO TOLSTOY (1828–1910)

• • •

The farmer's horse is never lame, never unfit to go. Never throws out curbs, never breaks down before or behind. . . . He does not paw and prance, and arch his neck, and bid the world admire his beauties . . . and when he is wanted, he can always do his work.
—ANTHONY TROLLOPE (1815–1882)

• • •

My name is Sunka Wakan, the Great Spirit Horse. I guess you could say that I am a very unique animal. . . . I have lived all these years because I have become a legend. You see, legends never die. They live on forever in the hearts of those who love to hear them.
—LINDA LITTLE WOLF, *GREAT SPIRIT HORSE*

• • •

He was a horse of goodly countenance, rather expressive of vigilance than fire; though an unnatural appearance of fierceness was thrown into it by the loss of his ears, which had been cropped pretty close to his head.
—AUGUSTUS B. LONGSTREET (1790–1870)

• • •

The sight of him did something to me I've never quite been able to explain. He was more than tremendous strength and speed and beauty of motion. He set me dreaming.
—WALT MOREY

• • •

His make and shape were so nearly perfect that he looked smaller at first glance. His shoulders were strong and well placed. . . . But perhaps the thing which struck you most about him was his proud and honest outlook. He was a beautiful horse.
—RICHARD FINDLAY, *THE DREAM*

• • •

The horse is a very gregarious creature.
—ARTHUR CONAN DOYLE (1859–1930)

• • •

Every day I pray to God to give me horses—wonderful horses—
to make me the best rider in England.
—ENID BAGNOLD (1880–1981)

• • •

We be of one blood, ye and I.
—RUDYARD KIPLING (1865–1936)

• • •

The cult of the horse as their idol is as central to their lives as
cocaine is to some and applause is to others.
—JUDITH KRANTZ

• • •

At least a half mile behind us was the Stable-Mart, the sorry
excuse for a stable, where I had the royal job of mucking out
stalls. Anything to be near horses.
—DANDI DALEY MACKALL

• • •

She could still hear Dad's words when he'd given Dove to her
five years earlier. "I picked him because he looks like you, Jan.
Both long-boned graceful. And you got the same look in your
eyes, like you were wanting something."
—C. S. ADLER, *ONE UNHAPPY HORSE*

• • •

The ability and intelligence is remarkable . . . Prince was able to walk the length of the furrow, between the growing potatoes, and when he was done you might never guess that he passed that way, so sure and careful was every footfall.
—PAUL HEINEY

• • •

The eyes, circled by his sad and beautiful darkness, were so sorrowful, lonely, gentle, and nobly tragic, that they killed all other emotions except love.
—T. H. WHITE

• • •

The smell was a mixture of hay and leather and—OK, maybe the faint odor of horse poop. But nothing had ever smelled as good.
—NANCY RUE

• • •

The bay filly . . . had more than beauty—she was so obviously the outcome of a splendid and selected ancestry. Even her manners were aristocratic.
—JOHN TAINTOR FOOTE

• • •

If Samantha had been born a horse, she would have been a plain bay.
—SUSAN NUSSER, *IN SERVICE TO THE HORSE*

• • •

I groomed the stallion until the desired change, because, comrades, I am a lover of white horses and have put into them that small quantity of strength that has remained to me.
—ISAAC BABEL (1894–1940)

• • •

My brother shall have a pair of horses with wings to fly among the clouds.
—RABINDRANATH TAGORE (1861–1941)

• • •

Whose only fit companion is his horse.
—WILLIAM COWPER

• • •

I saw a child who couldn't walk,
sit on a horse and laugh and talk; . . .
I saw a child who could only crawl,
mount a horse and sit up tall; . . .
I saw a child born into strife,
take up and hold the reins of life;
And the same child was heard to say,
"Thank you God for showing me the way."
—JOHN ANTHONY DAVIS

• • •

Inside the archway I paused. I love stables and horses and grooms, the cheerful sound of buckets, the heady smell of straw, the orderly fussiness of a saddle-room; always the same and ever different. The mind halts . . . at the moment when one sets foot within a stable-yard.
—MOLLY KEANE

• • •

My horse Abramka I endow to the regiment, I endow my horse for the remembrance of my soul.
—ISAAC BABEL

• • •

Magic was stabled at the sort of yard which should have warned Angela to beware . . . caution was nowhere to be found. She looked trustingly at the nondescript bay gelding produced for her inspection and saw only her dreams.
—DICK FRANCIS, *SPRING FEVER*

• • •

A woman never looks better than on horseback.
—JANE AUSTEN (1775–1817)

• • •

The two piebald horses, though they had shining coats and were obviously well cared-for, a fact Maria noticed at once because she adored horses, were old and stout and moved slowly.
—ELIZABETH GOUDGE, *THE LITTLE WHITE HORSE*

• • •

His neck is high and erect, his head replete with intelligence, his belly short, his back full, and his proud chest swells with hard muscles.
—VIRGIL (70–19 BC)

• • •

Buster began by breaking broncs, grubbing prickly pear, chopping firewood, wrangling horses, and held the cut when a big herd was being worked, a lowly job where much can be learned.
—THOMAS MCGUANE, *BUSTER*

• • •

I have never seen such a perfectly formed animal. Beautiful and graceful like a gazelle, he burned hot and wild with the deserts of Egypt in his soul.
—LYNN V. ANDREWS

• • •

Over the centuries the horse and his movement have been an inspiration to artists, poets, and writers.
—SUSAN E. HARRIS

• • •

And horses and mules and asses (hath He created) that ye may ride them, and for ornament. And he createth that which ye know not.
—THE KORAN

• • •

chapter six

"The Horse Is Never Wrong": Philosophies of Horsemanship

I don't want a horse that goes in a snaffle, I want one
that stops in a snaffle.
—STEVE PRICE

• • •

Realize that horsemanship is all about working on yourself,
not so much working on the horse. The horse is a rhythmical,
balanced, patient, trusting, and consistent animal. It's you who
needs to develop feel, timing, rhythm, balance, patience, consistency, and understanding.
—CRAIG CAMERON, *RIDE SMART*

• • •

The one great precept and practice in using a horse is this—never deal with him when you are in a fit of passion.
—XENOPHON

• • •

So many people nowadays don't know how to "read" a horse. I guess they are so used to a mechanized world that they don't think about a horse having ideas of his own.
—MARY TWELVEPONIES

• • •

The horse is never wrong.
—TOM DORRANCE

• • •

One of the cardinal rules of natural horsemanship is to ask the horse "as gently as possible, but as firmly as necessary." Notice that failure to get the response is not an option.
—DR. ROBERT M. MILLER AND RICK LAMB, *THE REVOLUTION IN HORSEMANSHIP*

• • •

The bottom line on what true horsemanship is: Communication. . . . How well can you get your horse to understand what it is you want him to do? How well can you get your horse to understand what it is you don't want him to do? That's horsemanship.
—CRAIG CAMERON, *RIDE SMART*

• • •

Because we are predators, ironically there is nothing "Natural" about "Natural Horsemanship." The term is used for want of a better phrase. Maybe creative or progressive horsemanship would be a better phraseology. Our unnatural relationship can be creatively developed between prey and predator by understanding their world.
—PETER FULLER

• • •

[A] horse never lies. The horse will be exactly as good as his human. When he has a choice, the horse will always make his own decision. And that decision will always be a reflection of you, the human.
—DENNIS REIS

• • •

I've started horses since I was twelve. . . . I've tried every physical means to contain my horse in an effort to keep from getting myself killed. I started to realize that things would come much easier for me once I learned why a horse does what he does.
—BUCK BRANNAMAN

• • •

The paradox of horses is that they do not *have* to carry us, but they agree to do so.
—TERESA TSIMMU MARTINO, *DANCER ON THE GRASS*

• • •

A definite purpose, like blinders on a horse, inevitably narrows its possessor's point of view.
—ROBERT FROST

• • •

Everything that's fun in life is dangerous. Horse races, for instance, are very dangerous. But attempt to design a safe horse and the result is a cow (an appalling animal to watch at the trotters.) And everything that isn't fun is dangerous too. It is impossible to be alive and safe.
—P. J. O'ROURKE, *REPUBLICAN PARTY REPTILE*

• • •

A good horse is hard to find.
—BOOTS REYNOLDS

• • •

Grab life by the reins.
—ANONYMOUS

• • •

One must get off one's horse over its head; to step off is merely weak.
—MAO TSE-TUNG

• • •

Horses have as much individuality and character as people.
—C. W. ANDERSON

• • •

But America is a great, unwieldly Body. Its Progress must be slow. . . . The fleetest Sailors must wait for the dullest and slowest. Like a Coach and six—the swiftest Horses must be slackened and the slowest quickened, that all may keep an even Pace.
—JOHN ADAMS (1735–1826)

• • •

Once a word leaves your mouth, you cannot chase it back even
with the swiftest horse.
—PROVERB

• • •

It doesn't matter to [our horses] if we have to be somewhere at
three o'clock. They don't. They cannot be forced into understanding or doing something faster just because we're running
out of time. This in itself is probably the biggest reason why
people have problems with their horses.
—MARK RASHID, *CONSIDERING THE HORSE: TALES
OF PROBLEMS SOLVED AND LESSONS LEARNED*

• • •

The tygers of wrath are wiser than the horses of instruction.
—WILLIAM BLAKE (1757–1827)

• • •

It left you a lot of time to hang around and listen to horse talk . . .
you'd find out about horses and men and pick up a lot of stuff
you could use all the rest of your life, if you had some sense and
salted down what you heard and felt and saw.
—SHERWOOD ANDERSON

• • •

Sickness comes on horseback, but goes away on foot.
—PROVERB

• • •

To me, horses and freedom are synonymous.
—VERYL GOODNIGHT

• • •

The horse, with beauty unsurpassed, strength immeasurable, and grace unlike any other, still remains humble enough to carry a man upon his back.
—AMBER SENTI

• • •

A cursed horse has a shining coat.
—CORSICAN PROVERB

• • •

The great advantage of a dialogue on horseback: it can be merged any minute into a trot or canter, and one might escape from Socrates himself in the saddle.
—GEORGE ELIOT

• • •

Horses change lives. They give our young people confidence and self esteem. They provide peace and tranquility to troubled souls—they give us hope!
—TONI ROBINSON

• • •

On the back of a horse you will find Paradise.
—STELLA A. WALKER

• • •

My horses are my friends, not my slaves.
—REINER KLIMKE

• • •

The only time some people work like a horse is when the boss rides them.
—GABRIEL HEATTER

• • •

It is the horse's gift to connect us with Heaven and our own footsteps.
—RONNI SWEET

• • •

Only when you see through the eyes of the horse, can you lead the dance of the mind.
—PETE SPATES

• • •

Industry is a better horse to ride than genius.
—WALTER LIPPMANN

• • •

A horse can lend its rider the speed and strength he or she lacks—but the rider who is wise remembers it is no more than a loan.
—PAM BROWN

• • •

My most trustworthy saddle horse . . . clamped on my upper leg . . . I threw him down on the ground . . . and put the tarp over him. I let him up two hours later; he thought I was the greatest man in the world, one he wouldn't think of biting. Horses only remember the end of the story.
—TOM MCGUANE

• • •

The only science that has ever existed in the world, relative to the breaking of horses, that has been of any value, is that true method which takes them in their native state, and improves their intelligence.
—JOHN RAREY(1827–1866), AMERICAN HORSE TRAINER

• • •

I can remember looking up at the sky and, however simplistic it may seem now, wondering if there was a God up there. . . . I find myself asking "big" questions when I'm . . . riding alone on horseback, and I'm here to tell you there is a God.
—BUCK BRANNAMAN

• • •

The cow, a large animal with horns on its head; its flesh and milk are excellent food. The horse, a large animal. Men sit upon his back and ride; he has no horns on his head.
—DAVID MALO (C. 1793–1853), *HAWAIIAN ANTIQUITIES*

• • •

The horse. Here is nobility without conceit, friendship without envy, beauty without vanity. A willing servant, yet never a slave.
—RONALD DUNCAN

• • •

Hay is for horses.
—AMERICAN PROVERB, A GENTLE REBUKE THAT ONE SHOULDN'T GREET ANOTHER WITH THE EXPRESSION "HEY, YOU!"

• • •

A beggar upon horseback lashes a beggar on foot.
—WILLIAM BUTLER YEATS

• • •

A man sentenced to death obtained a reprieve by assuring
the king he would teach his majesty's horse to fly within the
year. . . . "Within a year . . . the king may die, or I may die, or the
horse may die . . . who knows? Maybe the horse will learn to fly."
My philosophy is like that man's.
—BERNARD BARUCH

• • •

Its no use closing the stable door after the horse has bolted.
—JAPANESE SAYING

• • •

When your ship comes in, it just might be a horse.
—JAN JASION CROSS

• • •

If a horse won't eat it, I don't want to play on it.
—DICK ALLEN, ON ARTIFICIAL TURF

• • •

If you call a tail a leg, how many legs does a horse have? Four,
calling a tail a leg does not make it a leg.
—ABRAHAM LINCOLN (1809–1865)

• • •

Having heard the neigh of the horse, they were so enchanted with the sound, that they tried to imitate it; and, in trying to neigh, they forgot how to sing.
Moral: The desire for imaginary benefits often involves the loss or present blessings.
—AESOP

• • •

No hour of life is wasted that is spent in the saddle.
—WINSTON CHURCHILL

• • •

The ears never lie.
—DON BURT

• • •

There is no need of spurs when a horse is running away.
—PUBLILIUS SYRUS (C. FIRST CENTURY BC)

• • •

Horses lend us the wings we lack.
—PAM BROWN

• • •

Because a man is born in a stable that does not make him a horse.
—ARTHUR WELLESLEY (1769–1852)

• • •

Men without horses are nothing.
—JEREMY JAMES, *THE BYERLEY TURK: THE INCREDIBLE STORY OF THE WORLD'S FIRST THOROUGHBRED*

• • •

I say it is better to see a horse as a monster than to see it only as a slow substitute for a motor-car. If we have got into that state of mind about a horse as something stale, it is far better to be frightened of a horse because it is a good deal too fresh.
—G. K. CHESTERTON (1874–1936)

• • •

Nothing is more sacred as the bond between horse and rider . . . no other creature can ever become so emotionally close to a human as a horse. When a horse dies, the memory lives on because an enormous part of his owner's heart, soul, very existence dies also . . . but that can never be laid to rest, it is not meant to be.
—STEPHANIE M. THORN

• • •

I am not saying that you should not "love on" your horse. Go to it! But do it on your terms, not hers. You set the rules, and the most important rule is that she never invades your space. So many other good things in your relationship will flow from that simple rule.
—CHARLES WILHELM, *STARTING BABY JAZ*

• • •

No philosophers so thoroughly comprehend us as dogs and horses.
—HERMAN MELVILLE

• • •

We kept him until he died . . . and sat with him during the long last minutes when a horse comes closest to seeming human.
—C. J. MULLEN

• • •

For one to fly, one needs only to take the reins.
—MELISSA JAMES

• • •

There is no secret so close as that between a rider and his horse.
—ROBERT SMITH SURTEES (1803–1864)

• • •

Reckless automobile driving arouses the suspicion that much of the horse sense of the good old days was possessed by the horse.
—ANONYMOUS

• • •

In their eyes shine stars of wisdom and courage to guide men to the heavens.
—JODIE MITCHELL

• • •

There's nothing so good for the inside of a man as the outside of a horse.
—RONALD REAGAN

• • •

After God we owe it to the horses.
—ADOLF SCHREYER (1828–1899)

• • •

A dog looks up to a man, a cat looks down on a man, but a patient horse looks a man in the eye and sees him as an equal.
—ANONYMOUS

• • •

A ragged colt may prove a good horse. And so may an untoward slovenly boy prove a decent and useful man.
—JAMES KELLY

• • •

I have not permitted myself, gentlemen, to conclude that I am the best man in the country; but I am reminded, in this connection, of a story of an old Dutch farmer who remarked to a companion once that "it was not best to swap horses while crossing streams."
—ABRAHAM LINCOLN

• • •

The sun it was, ye glittering gods, ye took to make a horse.
—DIRGHATAMAS

• • •

Reason lies between the spur and the bridle.
—GEORGE HERBERT (1593–1633)

• • •

Horse sense is actually the animal's instinct for self-preservation.
—GORDON WRIGHT

• • •

Wild horses couldn't drag a secret out of a woman. However, women seldom have lunch with wild horses.
—IVERN BOYETT

• • •

Horses are the dolphins of the plains, the spirits of the wind; yet we sit astride them for the sake of being well-groomed, whereas they could have all the desire in the world to bolt, but instead, they adjust their speed and grace, only to please us, never to displease.
—LAUREN SALERNO

• • •

When a harvester grows weary of his work, it is said "He has the fatigue of the Horse." The first sheaf, called the "Cross of the Horse," is placed on a cross of boxwood in the barn, and the youngest horse on the farm must tread on it.
—SIR JAMES GEORGE FRAZER, *THE GOLDEN BOUGH*

• • •

Don't ride the high horse. The fall, when it comes, is hard.
—AMERICAN PROVERB

• • •

If God had intended man to walk, he would have given him four legs. Instead, he gave him two—one to put on either side of a horse.
—MONTANA RANCHER

• • •

The wagon rests in winter, the sleigh in summer, the horse never.
—YIDDISH PROVERB

• • •

What the colt learns in youth he continues in old age.
—FRENCH PROVERB

• • •

A horse with two heads wins no races.
—AMERICAN PROVERB

• • •

Many people have sighed for the "good old days" and regretted the "passing of the horse," but today, when only those who like horses own them, it is a far better time for horses.
—C. W. ANDERSON

• • •

Intimate acquaintance with the horse's knowledge . . . mark the faces of some older riders with the look that I have also seen on the faces of a few poets and thinkers, the incandescent gaze of unmediated awareness that some might be tempted to call innocence.
—VICKI HEARNE, *ADAM'S TASK*

• • •

Belief? What do I believe in? I believe in sun. In rock . . . and broom-tailed horses.
—EDWARD ABBEY

• • •

Keep five yards from a carriage, ten yards from a horse, and a hundred yards from an elephant; but the distance one should keep from a wicked man cannot be measured.
—INDIAN PROVERB

• • •

People on horses look better than they are. People in cars look worse than they are.
—MARYA MANNES

• • •

The primeval instincts of the horse are nowhere more pronounced than in the bond between the mare and the foal, for the maternal instinct is the strongest in nature. It is the instinct that ensures the survival of the species and determines the character of them and her attitude towards other horses and toward man.
—H. H. ISENBART

• • •

Horses and children, I often think, have a lot of the good sense there is in the world.
—JOSEPHINE DEMOTT ROBINSON

• • •

Heaven is high and earth wide. If you ride three feet higher above the ground than other men, you will know what that means.
—RUDOLF C. BINDING

• • •

A horse is the projection of peoples' dreams about themselves—strong, powerful, beautiful—and it has the capability of giving us escape from our mundane existence.
—PAM BROWN

• • •

Let us look beyond the ears of our own horses so that we may see the good in one another's.
—OLD EQUINE EXPRESSION

• • •

Men are not hanged for stealing horses but that horses may not be stolen.
—SIR GEORGE SAVILE (1726–1784)

• • •

In ceremonies of the horsemen, even the pawn must hold a grudge.
—BOB DYLAN

• • •

God first made Man. He thought better of it and made Woman. When he got time he made the Horse, which has the courage and spirit of Man and the beauty and grace of Woman.
—BRAZILIAN SAYING

• • •

A tree might be a show in Scotland as a horse in Venice.
—SAMUEL JOHNSON

• • •

The cat lets Man support her. But unlike the dog, she is no hand-licker. Furthermore, unlike Man's other good friend, the horse, the cat is no sweating serf of Man. The only labor she condescends to perform is to catch mice and rats, and that's fun.
—VANCE PACKARD

• • •

If a mule gets a leg caught in a barbed-wire fence, she will either figure out how to free herself without injury or will wait stoically and patiently for help. . . . A horse veterinarian once told me that if everyone rode mules she would soon be out of business.
—JOHN HAUER, *THE NATURAL SUPERIORITY OF MULES*

• • •

Do not confuse motion and progress. A rocking horse keeps moving, but does not make any progress.
—ALFRED MONTAPERT

• • •

We ought to do good to others as simply as a horse runs.
—MARCUS AURELIUS (121–180)

• • •

The only constant thing in life is change, and things can change rapidly when you're dealing with horses.
—PAT PARELLI

• • •

Quality is like buying oats. If you want nice, clean, fresh oats, you must pay a fair price. However, if you can be satisfied with oats that have already been through the horse . . . that comes a little cheaper.
—ANONYMOUS

• • •

Soft grass for an old horse.
—BULGARIAN PROVERB

• • •

A Hibernian sage once wrote that there are three things a man never forgets: The girl of his early youth, a devoted teacher, and a great horse.
—C. J. J. MULLEN

• • •

A horse is worth more than riches.
—SPANISH PROVERB

• • •

Good people get cheated, just as good horses get ridden.
—CHINESE PROVERB

• • •

Spending that many hours in the saddle gave a man plenty of time to think. That's why so many cowboys fancied themselves Philosophers.
—CHARLES M. RUSSELL (1864–1926)

• • •

A horse is simply a horse.
—AVICENNA (C. 980–1037)

• • •

A horse is a vain thing for safety.
—PSALMS 33:17

• • •

The horse is God's gift to mankind.
—ARABIAN PROVERB

• • •

The daughter who won't lift a finger in the house is the same child who cycles madly off in the pouring rain to spend all morning mucking out a stable.
—SAMANTHA ARMSTRONG

• • •

A Horseman should know neither fear, nor anger.
—JAMES RAREY

• • •

A nod is as good as a wink to a blind horse.
—IRISH PROVERB

• • •

Horsemanship through the history of all nations has been considered one of the highest accomplishments. You can't pass a park without seeing a statue of some old codger on a horse. It must be to his bravery, you can tell it's not to his horsemanship.
—WILL ROGERS

• • •

[Fate is] a little like a horse with a loose rein. It can meander calmly, or break into a gallop without warning, leaving you to hang on for dear life.
—*STAR TREK: THE NEXT GENERATION*

• • •

There is one respect in which beasts show real wisdom . . . their quiet, placid enjoyment of the present moment.
—ARTHUR SCHOPENHAUER (1788–1860)

• • •

From a workaday drudge, [the shetland pony] became a fun-loving playmate. No door was closed to him, for he had taught himself how to slide bolts, open gates, rattle latches. His long lips became expert at plucking caps from children's heads or handkerchiefs from pockets.
—MARGUERITE HENRY

• • •

No matter what you weigh, the little fellow is your equal on a horse.
—WILL ROGERS

• • •

Never were abilities so much below mediocrity so well rewarded; no, not when Caligula's horse was made Consul.
—JOHN RANDOLPH, REGARDING RICHARD RUSH'S APPOINTMENT AS SECRETARY OF THE TREASURY

• • •

Lend a horse, and you may have back his skin.
—ENGLISH PROVERB

• • •

What we are seeking so frantically elsewhere may turn out to be the horse we have been riding all along.
—HARVEY COX, *TURNING EAST*

• • •

The labor of women in the house, certainly, enables men to produce more wealth than they otherwise could; and in this way women are economic factors in society. But so are horses.
—CHARLOTTE P. GILMAN

• • •

When you hear hoof beats in Texas, think horses not zebras.
—ANONYMOUS

• • •

A man trying to sell a blind horse always praises its feet.
—GERMAN PROVERB

• • •

The hardest thing to do on a horse is nothing at all.
—ANONYMOUS

• • •

Don't spur a willing horse.
—PROVERB

• • •

Brooks too wide for our leaping, hedges far too high. Loads too heavy for our moving, burdens too cumbersome for us to bear. Distances far beyond our journeying. The horse gave us mastery.
—PAM BROWN

• • •

If an ass goes traveling it will not come home a horse.
—PROVERB

• • •

I can make a General in five minutes but a good horse is hard to replace.
—ABRAHAM LINCOLN

• • •

Animals do not admire each other. A horse does not admire its companion.
—ATTRIBUTED TO VARIOUS

• • •

The ox longs for the gaudy trappings of the horse; the lazy pack-horse would fain plough.
—PROVERB

• • •

Never gallop Pegasus to death.
—ALEXANDER POPE (1688–1744)

• • •

Don't approach a goat from the front, a horse from the back, or a fool from any side.
—JEWISH PROVERB

• • •

Hurry! At a gallop! To Paradise.
—PRINCESS LOUISE-MARIE OF FRANCE (1812–1850),
HER LAST WORDS BEFORE DYING

• • •

chapter seven

"And They're Off!": At the Track and On the Track

To me, [the Kentucky Derby] is the one assignment of the sports year which I would most deeply regret missing. It is a noisy, wearing, sleepless week of work and play and a fellow feels like a litter case coming home, and I love it.
—RED SMITH

• • •

One way to stop a runaway horse is to bet on him.
—ATTRIBUTED TO VARIOUS

• • •

The race is not always to the swift, nor the battle to the strong, but that's the way to bet.
—DAMON RUNYON (1884–1946)

• • •

Sadie's right, that track is crooked! Lora May, it isn't the track,
it's the horses. They fix things up amongst themselves.
—JOSEPH L. MANKIEWICZ, DIRECTOR OF *A LETTER
TO THREE WIVES*

• • •

I hope I break even, I need the money.
—JOE E. LEWIS, ON BETTING

• • •

A racehorse is an animal that can take several thousand people
for a ride at the same time.
—MARJORIE JOHNSON

• • •

The only way Breezing Along can lose the race is to have somebody shoot him at the quarter pole, and of course nobody is
shooting horses at the quarter pole at Hialeah, though many
citizens often feel like shooting horses at the half.
—DAMON RUNYON, *PICK THE WINNER*

• • •

Betting is the manure to which the enormous crop of horse-races
and racehorse breeding in this and other countries is to a large
extent due.
—RICHARD BLACKMORE

• • •

Racetrack! Well . . . what am I doin' here?"
—GROUCHO MARX

• • •

No horse can go as fast as the money you put on it.
—EARL WILSON

• • •

A horse that relieves himself on the track will relieve you of your money.
—C. N. RICHARDSON, *SMALL TRACK BETTING*

• • •

A man in passion rides a horse that runs away with him.
—THOMAS FULLER (1608–1661)

• • •

Beauty, delicacy and position—these were the foundations of courtly equestrianism
—HENNING EICHBERG

• • •

There is moreover something magnificent, a kind of majesty in his whole frame, which exalts his rider with pride as he outstrips the wind in his course.
—PAULUS JOVIUS

• • •

The rhythm of the ride carried them on and on, and she knew that the horse was as eager as she, as much in love with the speed and air and freedom.
—GEORGESS MCHARGUE

• • •

In the saddle is heaven on earth.
—ANONYMOUS

• • •

We were gamblers . . . whether we admit it or not. What other sort of person would stake a dollar bill on an animal that runs on one toe at a time.
—SALLY JENKINS

• • •

A tout is a guy who goes around the race track giving out tips on the races, if he can find anybody who will listen to his tips, especially suckers, and a tout is nearly always broke. If he is not broke, he is by no means a tout, but a handicapper, and is respected by one and all.
—DAMON RUNYON

• • •

A mostly British expression urging someone to stick to the thing he knows best, "horses for courses" comes from the horse racing world, where it is widely assumed that some horses race better on certain courses than on others.
—ROBERT HENDRICKSON, *ENCYCLOPEDIA OF WORD AND PHRASE ORIGINS*

• • •

"I lived so close to Aqueduct that I would slip under the fence and do my running right on the track . . . "
—EDWARD L. BOWEN, *NASHUA*

• • •

The American male, at the peak of his physical powers and appetites, driving 160 big white horses across the scenery of an increasingly hopeless society, with weekend money in his pocket and with little prior exposure to trouble and tragedy, personifies "an accident going to happen."
—JOHN SLOAN DICKEY

• • •

If you bet on a horse, that's gambling. If you bet you can make three spades, that's entertainment. If you bet cotton will go up three points, that's business. See the difference ?
—BLACKIE SHERROD

• • •

Making a choice is like backing a horse—in a hundred years, they may decide you picked wrongly.
—EDWARD CARPENTER

• • •

The horse I bet on was so slow, the jockey kept a diary of the trip.
—HENNY YOUNGMAN

• • •

If you have any questions, I'll try to answer them. If it's not inconvenient, I might even tell you the truth . . . Ocala's my assistant, but don't bother him, he's a son of a bitch. And try to stay out of the way. I'm a working horse trainer, not a . . . tourist destination.
—P. G. JOHNSON

• • •

The Oracle looks at the book . . . no one . . . ventures to speak . . .
'Well . . . of course there's only one in it—if he's wanted' . . . No
one likes to expose . . . ignorance by asking which horse he refers
to as the 'only one in it'; and the Oracle goes on to deal out some
more wisdom in a loud voice.
—A. B. "BANJO" PATERSON, *THE ORACLE*

• • •

Everyone knows that horse racing is carried out mainly for the
delight and profit of fools, ruffians, and thieves.
—GEORGE GISSING (1857–1903)

• • •

There are times when you catch glimpses of the racetrack . . .
elegant and formal, a universe of bright surfaces where honor,
decorum, and order prevail.
—ERIC RACHLIS, BLOSSOM LEFCOURT, AND BERT
MORGAN, *HORSE RACING: THE GOLDEN AGE OF THE
TRACK*

• • •

Lord Hippo suffered fearful loss,
By putting money on a horse;
Which he believed, if it were pressed,
Would run faster than the rest.
—HILAIRE BELLOC (1870–1953)

• • •

And so there I was, sitting up in the grandstand . . . looking down
on the swipes coming out with their horses . . . I liked . . . sitting
up there and feeling grand. . . .
—SHERWOOD ANDERSON

• • •

No, I'm not a horse bettor. Every once in a while somebody will give me a sure thing and of course it's not.
—M. EMMET WALSH

• • •

I would come to look upon such mornings at the racetrack as my strongest ties to earth and place, my strongest link to the kind of heritage I would read about in the library.
—CAREY WINFREY, *TIP ON A LOST RACE*

• • •

Lady Godiva put everything she had on a horse.
—W. C. FIELDS

• • •

The only decent people I ever saw at the racecourse were horses.
—JAMES JOYCE (1882–1941)

• • •

When I started playing the horses and trying to comprehend the mysteries of the game, I thought I was searching for great, immutable truths. I thought there must be a set of principles that governed the outcome of races and were waiting to be discovered.
—ANDREW BEYER, *THE WINNING HORSEPLAYER*

• • •

The best horse is not necessarily the best bet. In order to evaluate a bet, we must know . . . the probability of winning the bet, and the payoff if we win. . . . It is the relationship between these two factors which determines the expected return of the bet.
—STEVEN L. BRECHER, *BEATING THE RACES WITH A COMPUTER*

• • •

A beginning horseplayer picking a cold trifecta is like a guy who's
never held a dart shooting three straight bull's-eyes.
—TED MCCLELLAND, *HORSEPLAYERS*

• • •

Horses have never hurt anyone yet, except when they bet on
them.
—STUART CLOETE (1897–1976)

• • •

Thursday afternoon Tricksy Wilcox scratched his armpit absent-
mindedly and decided Claypits wasn't worth backing in the
2:30. [Later that day] Tricksy watched Claypits win the 2:30 with
insulting ease and drank down his dented self-esteem with the
last of the beer.
—DICK FRANCIS, *A ROYAL RIP-OFF AT KINGDOM
HILL*

• • •

There he lives from noon to five pm on every day when there is
racing, ceaselessly receiving scraps of paper stating that someone
(for initials only are used) is eager to wager 2s 6d on Blue Moon
in the two-thirty pm race at Wye.
—C. C. L. BROWNE, *THE INSIDE VIEW*

• • •

You Can Eat Your Betting Money, but Never Bet Your Eating
Money.
—SIGN IN MANY RACETRACK CAFETERIAS

• • •

From New York City, you drive north for about 175 miles, turn left on Union Avenue, and go back one hundred years.
—RED SMITH, WHEN ASKED FOR DIRECTIONS TO SARATOGA RACE COURSE

• • •

The racing people were busy discussing prospects for the final day. The first day's racing had been interesting; some long shots had come home, and a few among the crowd in the lounge were conscious as they talked of fatter, heavier wallets hanging in their inside pockets.
—MAURICE GEE, *THE LOSERS*

• • •

Who makes the most money? Horse bettors first, followed by sports bettors. Then poker, golf hustlers, and blackjack and backgammon players.
—RICHARD W. MUNCHKIN IN *GAMBLING WIZARDS*

• • •

This is the only place where the windows clean the people.
—JOE E. LEWIS, ON RACETRACKS

• • •

Saratoga is forever known as the "Graveyard of Champions."
—BILL HELLER, *SARATOGA TALES: GREAT HORSES, FEARLESS JOCKEYS, SHOCKING UPSETS AND INCREDIBLE BLUNDERS AT AMERICA'S LEGENDARY RACE TRACK*

• • •

There are not immutable truths, no absolute rights and wrongs, because the only meaningful measure of any handicapping method is its profitability. Certain systems may produce profits for a while, but as the betting public catches on to them the odds drop and the systems eventually cease to work.
—ANDREW BEYER, *THE WINNING HORSEPLAYER*

• • •

The racetrack is strikingly romantic. It has a kind of grandeur, even an epic quality. The horses, too, are blessed with a heroic dimension.
—ERIC RACHLIS, BLOSSOM LEFCOURT, AND BERT MORGAN, *HORSE RACING: THE GOLDEN AGE OF THE TRACK*

• • •

On arrival at the course, the Oracle is in great form. Attended by his string of satellites, he plods from stall to stall staring at the horses. Their names are printed in big letters on the stalls, but the Oracle doesn't let that stop his display of knowledge.
—A. B. "BANJO" PATERSON, *THE ORACLE*

• • •

Keeping horses in order to have a bet is not a job for a poor man.
—COLIN DAVY, *THE MAJOR*

• • •

Friday afternoon, having pinched a tenner from his wife's holiday fund in the best teapot, Tricksy Wilcox went to the races.
—DICK FRANCIS, *A ROYAL RIP-OFF AT KINGDOM HILL*

• • •

Well, I am not going to bother you the details of the race, but this horse Breezing Along is nowhere. In fact, he is so far back that I do not recollect seeing him finish, because by the time the third horse in the field crosses the line, Hot Horse Herbie and me are on our way back to town.
—DAMON RUNYON

• • •

The horse racing handicapping system does not reward brilliance, it punishes it. If tennis were run along these lines, Roger Federer would start his matches two sets down. But tennis is not a betting sport in the way that racing is. Nothing is.
—CLARE BALDING

• • •

Chuck and I felt our very presence among the drunken, happy hordes of the Churchill Downs infield was a victory, no matter what happened for us at the betting windows.
—ELIZABETH MITCHELL, *THREE STRIDES BEFORE THE WIRE*

• • •

Horse sense is what keeps horses from betting on what people will do.
—RAYMOND NASH, *PEARLS OF WISDOM*

• • •

A longshot wins a race. A disappointed bettor consults his Form and discovers that the longshot had been timed at 36 seconds in a breezing three-furlong workout a couple of days ago. No other horse in the race had worked so rapidly so recently. Powie! A new system is born!
—TOM AINSLIE, *AINSLIE'S COMPLETE GUIDE TO THOROUGHBRED RACING*

• • •

"I never bet," I ses, "an' I take no interest in horse-racing' an', moreover," I ses, "she cant give Bountiful Boy seven pounds over a mile an' a quarter."
—EDGAR WALLACE

• • •

Never bet on a sure thing unless you can afford to lose.
—ANONYMOUS

• • •

Anything can happen in a handicap . . . All good horses might fall—you never know.
—DICK FRANCIS

• • •

The grandstand had the empty, aimless feeling of a shopping mall. I spread out my program on a table and ran my eyes across lines of statistics . . . I had learned to handicap—to dope out the winners of a horse race—when I was just a small child.
—TED MCCLELLAND, *HORSEPLAYERS*

• • •

In 1999 *Sports Illustrated* named Saratoga Race Course "as one of the Top Ten sporting venues in the world." Two years later, *ESPN Magazine* called Saratoga "the loveliest racetrack in the country."
—BILL HELLER, *SARATOGA TALES: GREAT HORSES, FEARLESS JOCKEYS, SHOCKING UPSETS AND INCREDIBLE BLUNDERS AT AMERICA'S LEGENDARY RACE TRACK*

• • •

At the track, the odds are not set by the house, as they are in a casino. They're set by the amount of money bet on each horse. The more money bet, the lower the odds. This is known as pari-mutuel wagering.
—TED MCCLELLAND, *HORSEPLAYERS*

• • •

It is during the last race meeting at Saratoga, and one evening I am standing out under the elms in front of the Grand Union Hotel thinking what a beautiful world it is, to be sure, for what do I do in the afternoon at the track but grab myself a piece of a ten-to-one shot.
—DAMON RUNYON

• • •

I once asked my dad to tell me about his life. "Pretty simple," he answered. "Went to the races, got married, got divorced; went to the races, got married, got divorced; went to the races, got married, got divorced. Went to the races."
—VICTORIA VANDERBILT

• • •

Every gambler relies on such gimmicks. My own trick is never to hold on to a losing ticket, for fear it will contaminate my aura and keep me from ever cashing a bet.
—BILL BARICH, *DREAMING*

• • •

Playing the races appears to be the one business in which men believe they can succeed without special study, special talent, or special exertion.
—*RACING MAXIMS AND METHODS OF "PITTSBURGH PHIL"*

• • •

Poor devil, poor devil, he's best gone out of a life where he rides his rocking-horse to find a winner.
—D. H. LAWRENCE

• • •

Perhaps he should delay his return home and we should go to the Derby, because surely that was the lesson of life: that, within reason, you never regret what you do, but only what you fail to do.
—ELIZABETH MITCHELL, *THREE STRIDES BEFORE THE WIRE*

• • •

Horse racing is animated roulette.
—ROGER KAHN

• • •

It has been my custom . . . to rise at dawn and to proceed to the track to see the horses train . . . one can learn . . . if one has ears and eyes. It is . . . a beautiful sight . . . to see the horses jogging around the track, past the deserted grandstand, more beautiful than a picture.
—J. P. MARQUAND

• • •

[A] bet is the placing of a wager on a "contender" to finish first in the race. This is the "win bet." Other bets are "quinella," "exacta," "trifecta" or "triple," "daily double," "pick three."
—M. PAUL ANDERSON, *WAGERING TO WIN*

• • •

I'd been a fan of racing all my life . . . since my grandfather took me to see the flamingos in the infield at beautiful old Hialeah in Florida. I'd never thought about being a sportswriter, but it seemed natural enough to write about a horse race.
—MAX WATMAN, *RACE DAY*

• • •

The earliest owner of Saratoga Race Course was a boxer-turned-gambler named James Morrissey. Morrissey developed the track for a specific crowd, making it attractive to the high rollers—he even camouflaged the gambling that was present by naming the casino the "Club House."
—NANCY STOUT, *HOMESTRETCH*

• • •

The weeks passed, Pennyfeather . . . humorously thanked his stars that he was old enough not to risk his bank balance on anything with four legs.
—J. C. SQUIRE, *THE DEAD CERT*

• • •

Many of the early tracks were tracks in the same way raisins can be considered fruits—technically, and only in a manner of speaking.
—BERT SUGAR AND CORNELL RICHARDSON, *HORSE SENSE: AN INSIDE LOOK AT THE SPORT OF KINGS*

• • •

No horse goes as fast as the money you bet on him.
—ANONYMOUS

• • •

Nobody has ever bet enough on a winning horse.
—AMERICAN PROVERB

• • •

One of the worst things that can happen to you in life is to win a bet on a horse at an early age.
DANNY MCGOORTY

• • •

Ascot is so exclusive that it is the only racecourse in the world where the horses own the people.
—ART BUCHWALD

• • •

Saratoga . . . was always embraced for its summer racing—so much so that summer racing at Saratoga became an institution.
—NANCY STOUT, *HOMESTRECTH*

• • •

A racetrack is a place where the human race is secondary.
—ANONYMOUS

• • •

He had seen almost nothing of a horse; his racecourse hours were spent ferreting among a bawling, perspiring crowd. . . . He never went near a race-meeting . . . yet his conversation seldom deviated for more than a minute at a time from that physically unknown animal the horse.
—JOHN GALSWORTHY, *HAD A HORSE*

• • •

When Protagonist rallied to beat Stonewalk by two lengths, I could not explain the outcome of the race in any way that was consistent with my own philosophy.
—ANDREW BEYER

• • •

A profit at the race track isn't a profit until you spend it somewhere else.
—CHARLES CARROLL, *HANDICAPPING SPEED*

• • •

He is called Hot Horse Herbie because he can always tell you
about a horse that is so hot it is . . . all readied up to win a race,
although sometimes Herbie's hot horses turn out to be so cold
they freeze everybody within fifty miles of him.
—DAMON RUNYON, *PICK THE WINNER*

• • •

Betting the ponies is done in various methodical ways by profes-
sionals, haphazardly by some enthusiasts, and often in a rather
bizarre fashion by others just out for a day's lark.
—COOKY MCCLUNG, *HORSEFOLK ARE DIFFERENT*

• • •

After all, if you remove the gambling, where is the fun in
watching a bunch of horses being whipped by midgets?
—IAN O'DOHERTY

• • •

The quaint custom of moving an entire household from the
city to a cooler place in the country during the hottest month of
summer brought racing fans to Saratoga. . . . People flocked to
Saratoga for the cool pine forests of the Adirondack Muntains
and the therapeutic mineral springs.
—NANCY STOUT, *HOMESTRECTH*

• • •

If it can happen, it happens at Saratoga.
—GEORGE CASSIDY

• • •

There are a million miles of difference between the words "win" and "beat." We don't ever allow the word "beat" on this farm. Because when you start talking about beating someone, you've lost your concentration. You're thinking about the opposition.
—HELEN CRABTREE

• • •

He disliked looking back in a race because this action was apt to make one's horse unbalanced, but in this case the knowledge thus gained would make a difference to the way in which he would jump the fence.
—RICHARD FINDLAY, *THE DREAM*

• • •

Competitive riding should be classical riding at its best.
—CHARLES DE KUNFFY

• • •

When you're riding, only the race in which you're riding is important.
—BILL SHOEMAKER

• • •

I hope you'll always love Thoroughbred racing and the Kentucky Derby. And never feel embarrassed about shedding a tear or two when "My Old Kentucky Home" is played at Churchill Downs on the first Saturday in May. I wouldn't have it any other way.
—BILLY REED, *MY FAVORITE DERBY STORIES*

• • •

The hot thing kicked . . . as we went down to the start. It jumped the first fence so fast that I did not have time to fall off. At the second it . . . turned itself into a . . . corkscrew. I went sailing away. The ground came up to meet me with an almighty bang.
—JOHN WELCOME, *MY FIRST WINNER*

• • •

The Whitbread Gold Cup, scheduled for six weeks ahead was the last race of the season. To have a horse fit to run it, and to have Derek Roberts ride it, seemed to be the pinnacle in her racing life that she had never envisaged. Her horizons, her joy, expanded like flowers.
—DICK FRANCIS, *SPRING FEVER*

• • •

Losers walking around with money in their pockets are always dangerous, not to be trusted. Some horse always reaches out and grabs them.
—BILL BARICH, *LAUGHING IN THE HILLS*

• • •

They were off like rockets as the barrier shot, and the bay filly flashed into the lead. Her slender legs seemed to bear her as though on the breast of the wind. She did not run—she floated—yet the gap between herself and her struggling schoolmates grew even wider.
—JOHN TAINTOR FOOTE, *BLISTER*

• • •

When I started riding, winning wasn't thought to be all that important. It was simply something that happened if you worked hard . . . *Having fun* was the important thing.
—WILLIAM STEINKRAUS

• • •

Sometimes I make the wrong move and it turns out to be the right move. The point is you have to have someone between the shafts. Horses are all about the same. It's just some are faster than others. I'm out there to win money. Not for the love of this or that. The money.
—HERVE FILION

• • •

The sun has not yet risen over Saratoga Race Course, but the glory of impending dawn paints the sky lavender. Fog wanders the infield in wisps, slipping over the inside rail and onto the track. While the town lies silent, most occupants asleep, the track awakens.
—BARBARA D. LIVINGSTON, *BARBARA D. LIVINGSTON'S SARATOGA*

• • •

Not all jockeys loved horses; for many, they were merely animals, tools for making a living and maybe getting rich. But Jimmy Winkfield not only loved them, he needed them.
—ED HOTALING, *WINK: THE INCREDIBLE LIFE AND EPIC JOURNEY OF JIMMY WINKFIELD*

• • •

I love watching a good horse do what he's bred to do—I guess that's what I like the most about it. And I love to see good athletes do what they're bred to do.
—WILFORD BRIMLEY

• • •

There appears to be no immunity to this dangerous germ. If as a parent you observe your little precious pick up a toy horse, make galloping noises, and plop it over a block, screaming "Win!" you've had it. The jumping rider's disease is loose in your house.
—RAYMOND WOOLFE JR.

• • •

The best horse doesn't always win the race.
—IRISH PROVERB

• • •

"The fastest two minutes in sports."
—ON THE KENTUCKY DERBY

• • •

You win, you're happy; you lose, you're disappointed—but don't let either one carry you away.
—BUSTER WELCH

• • •

Like any race, once the Derby starts, any horse can win.
—FUNNY CIDE TEAM AND BARRY MOSER, *A HORSE NAMED FUNNY CIDE*

• • •

A winning formula. A very simple one, much favored by trainers at the race track, is to have the best horse.
—WILLIAM STEINKRAUS

• • •

Those sweet young things performed . . . every lawless act known to the equine brain. They reared. They plunged. They bucked. They spun. They surged together. They scattered like startled quail. I heard squeals, and saw vicious shiny hoofs lash out in every direction.
—JOHN TAINTOR FOOTE

• • •

Well out by herself she was, an' there she kept right along the straight to the distance. There was no chance of the others catchin' her, an' they were easin' up when suddenly from the rails came a report like the snap of a whip, an' the Belle staggered, swerved, an' went down all of a heap.
—EDGAR WALLACE

• • •

One of the few names that I remember was Jimmy Winkfield. My grandfather called him "Wink." He would often say, "Boy, before there was a Jackie Robinson or a Jessie Owens, we . . . had a sport where we made the difference. Horse racing!"
—C. N. RICHARDSON

• • •

Because we have the best hay and the best oats and the best horses.
—COL. SIR HARRY LLEWELLYN, ON WHY THE BRITISH SHOW JUMPING TEAM WAS SO SUCCESSFUL IN THE 1952 OLYMPICS

• • •

A key winning component that can even compensate partially for some other deficiencies is simply to have the best competitive attitude.
—WILLIAM STEINKRAUS

• • •

Some athletes don't care what kind of shoes they wear, or how many fans they have. They don't even care that they're on television from coast to coast. They just want to run.
—ANONYMOUS, ON HORSES

• • •

The only trouble with that horse is that it doesn't like jockeys. Once it's thrown its jockey it goes like the wind.
—HENRY CECIL

• • •

The only sport I'm not interested in is horse racing. That's because I don't know the horses personally.
—NAT KING COLE

• • •

Seemed to be some kind of prehistoric throwback, a living legend
of the days when horses were hunted, when fear and hunger
ruled their lives. In a classy stable of calm, earnest animals,
Sunday Silence was Al Capone singing in the Vienna Boys Choir.
—JAY HOVDEY

• • •

Trainer Michael Matz ignored Kentucky Derby tradition by
sending a good horse to Churchill Downs after not having raced
him in the previous five weeks . . . no horse in half a century had
won the Derby after a five-week layoff. The wailing persisted
until Barbaro rolled to victory by six and a half lengths.
—TIM LAYDEN

• • •

There is no feeling that equals the one that overcomes you on
your way to the winner's circle . . . All of the joy and heartache
that accompany raising a racehorse can never be expressed in
words, but it all comes together in that tiny piece of dirt.
—CAROL WADE KELLY

• • •

Thoroughbred: This is the racehorse *par excellence.*
—COLIN VOGEL, *COMPLETE HORSE CARE MANUAL*

• • •

Everyone talks about the last quarter-mile of the Derby, but the
race is really won in the first quarter-mile, between the gate and
the first turn.
—KENT DESORMEAUX

• • •

The child who is fortunate enough to be associated with horses during his formative years can look back on fond memories, and those who continue to ride, hunt, or show during their lifetime seldom experience anything more gratifying than the thrill of winning their first ribbon.
—STEPHEN O. HAWKINS

• • •

Helping horses to achieve their full potential and working to achieve your own are satisfying and fulfilling, and if you can come close to accomplishing this, winning as such will take care of itself.
—WILLIAM STEINKRAUS

• • •

Wink guided his colt along the north side of the grandstand, trotted onto the track, and got a thrill known to only a few hundred humans before him. It was May 3, 1900, and he was riding at Churchill Downs on Derby Day.
—ED HOTALING, *WINK: THE INCREDIBLE JOURNEY LIFE AND EPIC JOURNEY OF JIMMY WINKFIELD*

• • •

We are led into the starting gate. . . . Then my horse is still. The bell rings, the doors fly open, and with an incredible lurch that all but throws me from the saddle, we are off.
—CAREY WINFREY

• • •

Most good horses know when they'd won: filled their lungs and raised their heads with pride. Some were definitely depressed when they lost. Guilt they never felt, nor shame not regret nor compassion.
—DICK FRANCIS

• • •

A horse gallops with his lungs,
Perseveres with his heart,
And wins with his character.
—FEDERICO TESIO (1869–1954)

• • •

It is not best that we should all think alike; it is a difference of opinion that makes horse races.
—MARK TWAIN

• • •

Remember that the horse that finishes a neck ahead wins the race.
—ANONYMOUS

• • •

To finish is to win.
—ENDURANCE RIDING MOTTO

• • •

The harrowing uncertainty of the turf.
—RED SMITH

• • •

A horse never runs so fast as when he has other horses to catch up and outpace.
—OVID

• • •

An exhibitor went up to a horse show judge to complain about being placed below someone who made some sort of mistake . . . The judge's explanation: "The other guy did it better wrong than you did it right."
—ANONYMOUS

• • •

I let the horse do the work. I guide him. If the horse gets beat, it's not my fault. If he wins, it's not my fault.
—HERVE FILION

• • •

Don't fuss too much about your start. It's no odds getting off in a tear-away. What you got to do is jump round and jump clean and go as fast as you can when you know what you're doing. But wait till you know what you're doing before you hurry.
—ENID BAGNOLD

• • •

It's simply my creed that an executive of a race track might bring certain censure upon the sport by owning horses that campaign at his track, or by betting on the outcome of races at a track where he is supervisor.
—MATT WINN (1861–1949)

• • •

I had acquired some small . . . proficiency in the business of sitting a horse at racing pace over fences and making a pretence of staying on him if things went wrong. This had not been achieved without a considerable amount of bruising and breaking, hard work, dedication, disappointment, toil, and sweat.
—JOHN WELCOME

• • •

I was more nervous than when I played before 55,000 at Old Trafford.
—MICK QUINN, EX-SOCCER PLAYER ON SENDING OUT HIS FIRST RUNNER AS A HORSE TRAINER AT SOUTHWELL IN 1997

• • •

He trots down the straight to win the race. Lord, Cap, you should have heard the people cheer! I never heard anything like it, not even on Derby Day.
—COLIN DAVY

• • •

A few years ago, I gave an interview in which I referred to sport as a crucible. My point was that if things are done correctly, the heat and pressure generated within the crucible of competition should burn away all that is base and false, leaving only the pure and true.
—JAMES C. WOFFORD

• • •

Julie Krone rides Thoroughbreds as well as anyone. . . . She rides the way Bill Shoemaker rode. Waiting, watching, waiting for the time to move. Racetrackers call it sitting chilly.
—DAVE KINDRED

• • •

He had watched her . . . when she raced, but only from the . . . stands. . . . Up close . . . he'd begun to realize . . . [s]he had the uncanny ability to seem calm and excited at the same time. Perfectly at ease, and . . . eager, intense, wired. He had never seen that in a horse . . . or . . . in a person either.
—JANE SCHWARTZ, *RUFFIAN: BURNING FROM THE START*

• • •

Anybody can win unless there happens to be a second entry.
—GEORGE ADE

• • •

He should have lived with the wild horses of the prairie where he could have been boss. There the issue would have been settled quickly; he would have ruled or died. . . . Finally he did what they asked but not because he had changed his mind.
—J. A. ESTES, ON THROUGHBRED RACEHORSE DISPLAY

• • •

When you peel back the layers of racing, you are left with the horse and the groom.
—CHARLSIE CANTEY

• • •

One of the wonderful things about our equestrian sport is the great diversity of breeds and disciplines.
—HALLIE MCEVOY, *HORSE SHOW JUDGING FOR BEGINNERS*

• • •

I don't think of Julie as a girl. I think of her as a rider. A great rider. She has courage that cannot be measured.
—NICK ZITO, ON JULIE KRONE

• • •

Actors are the jockeys of literature. Others supply the horses, the plays, and we simply make them run.
—RALPH RICHARDSON

• • •

The spirited horse, which will try to win the race of its own accord, will run even faster if encouraged.
—OVID

• • •

A cutting competition is nothing more than a contest of "oh shits" and "attaboys." And the person with more attaboys is the winner.
—BUSTER WELCH

• • •

I had never grown up around horses, never owned a horse, never knew anyone who owned horses. To conceive of the dream, as I did, of . . . owning champion racehorses was truly ludicrous. Yet I was driven to make it happen.
—GEORGE ROWAND

• • •

Every horseman and horsewoman alive . . . wants to believe that among the babies in the barn that are just beginning racing careers there is *the* one. . . . The magical equine athlete who in the springtime of his third year on this earth can . . . win one— or, better, all three—of the races that make up the Triple Crown.
—JOE DRAPE, *THE RACE FOR THE TRIPLE CROWN: HORSES, HIGH STAKES, AND ETERNAL HOPE*

• • •

The wild horse race was usually no race at all but a kind of maniacal musical chairs played with mustangs.
—MONTY ROBERTS, *THE MAN WHO LISTENS TO HORSES*

• • •

The bell rang, an' there was a yell. "They're off!"
—EDGAR WALLACE

• • •

The best horse usually wins, but not always.
—TOM AINSLIE, *AINSLIE'S COMPLETE GUIDE TO THOROUGHBRED RACING*

• • •

As distance shows a horse's strength, so time reveals a person's heart.
—CHINESE PROVERB

• • •

I've had one hundred people tell me, "You shouldn't do this. You don't have the money, you don't have the talent, you're not going to make it." There are always doubters, but I don't worry about what other people think.
—NONA GARSON

• • •

Politics is like a racehorse. A good jockey must know how to fall with the least possible danger.
—ÉDOUARD HERRIOTT (1872–1957)

• • •

Not only did Barbaro win the Derby, he demolished what was supposed to be one of the toughest fields in years. The six-and-a-half-length winning margin was the largest since 1946, when Assault won by eight lengths and went on to sweep the Triple Crown.
—SI.COM

• • •

Barbaro left no doubt he was the class of an already classy group.
—MARYJEAN WALL

• • •

Horses and jockeys mature earlier than people—which is why horses are admitted to racetracks at the age of two, and jockeys before they are old enough to shave.
—DICK BEDDOES

• • •

When I turned him loose, he took off like a rocket.
—EDGAR PRADO, BARBARO'S JOCKEY

• • •

In practice do things as perfectly as you can; in competition, do what you have to do.
—WILLIAM STEINKRAUS

• • •

There are few things I enjoy more in this world than watching Thoroughbreds compete . . . we all try to catch a flash of brilliance here or there, a hint of promise that tomorrow big dreams will come true, that the horses we're watching today will be champions.
—MICHAEL COMPTON

• • •

If you're lucky enough to draw a good horse, you still have to ride him, then the next ones. So it's probably 80 percent luck and 20 percent skill.
—CHRIS LEDOUX

• • •

Took the next fence like a rocket. I shook the reins at him. Away we went down the straight with myself giving the best imitation I could of riding a finish. No challenge came. The judge's box flashed. It all seemed too easy. It was.
—JOHN WELCOME

• • •

The Oxford English Dictionary defines "classic," from the French *classique*, and Latin *classicus*, as meaning "of the first rank or authority," which gets its racing sense exactly; but the word is not used to describe races until 1885 . . . in the phrase "classic races."
—GERALD HAMMOND

• • •

Buck thought of the crowds that cheered her every time she ran. If only they could see her now. She was a towering filly, and had always looked magnificent on those bright afternoons when she raced. . . . But at night . . . she was even more striking.
—JANE SCHWARTZ, *RUFFIAN: BURNING FROM THE START*

• • •

I imagined galloping down the stretch. I could hear the thundering hooves and the roaring crowd. I imagined them laying the roses across my lap. It was a great feeling of romance.
—JULIE KRONE

• • •

We were all shocked. The heart of the average horse weighs about nine pounds. This was almost twice the average size, and a third larger than any equine heart I'd ever seen. All the chambers and valves were normal. It was just larger. I think it told us why he was able to do what he did.
—DR. THOMAS SWECZEK, AFTER PERFORMING AN AUTOPSY ON SECRETARIAT

• • •

How the horse dominated the mind of the early races, especially of the Mediterranean! You were a lord if you had a horse.
—D. H. LAWRENCE

• • •

[A] dark horse which had never been thought of, and which the careless St. James had never even observed in the list, rushed past the grand stand in sweeping triumph.
—BENJAMIN DISRAELI (1805–1881)

• • •

Let's talk about the death of Seabiscuit the other night. It isn't mawkish to say, there was a racehorse, a horse that gave race fans as much pleasure as any that has ever lived and one that will be remembered as long and as warmly.
—RED SMITH

• • •

After one of them has won the Derby, any breeding expert can sit down and show you just why he won, from his pedigree. The only trouble is, the expert can't do it before the race.
—PHIL CHINN

• • •

Monastic Calm beat the other quad by twenty lengths, and was never going more than half-speed neither.
—COLIN DAVY, *THE GOOD THINGS*

• • •

You have to bear in mind that Mr. Autry's favorite horse was named Champion. He ain't ever had one called Runner Up.
—GENE MAUCH

• • •

Since the earliest of years, humans have studied what they call "common sense." We in horsedom call it "horse sense." What it means is that things are not always as they appear. Try reading the *Daily Racing Form* and picking the winners, and you'll know what I mean.
—ROBERT L. MERZ

• • •

The archives of statistics . . . demonstrate that the most certain way of breeding stakes performers is to send stakes-winning and/or producing mares to proven, top-echelon sires. Done repetitively, this will improve the odds of getting a good horse.
—TIMOTHY T. CAPPS, *SPECTACULAR BID*

• • •

He's diseased with speed.
—JOHN TAINTOR FOOTE

• • •

On the morning of the Belmont Stakes he had burst from the
barn like a stud horse going to the breeding shed.
—WILLIAM NACK

• • •

If the horse is used for the purpose of the rider's ego in winning
competition points, dressage is no longer an art but an abuse of a
generous long-suffering animal.
—SALLY O'CONNOR

• • •

It is damnably hard to know for certain which horse will win . . .
but a trainer, jockey, or groom can often be very sure indeed that
a horse will lose.
—MATTHEW ENGEL

• • •

She was perfect. . . . Always first. Always on the lead. Perfect.
—JANE SCHWARTZ, *RUFFIAN: BURNING FROM THE
START*

• • •

The first time he saw Seabiscuit, the colt was walking through the
fog at five in the morning. Smith would say later that the horse
looked right through him, as if to say, "What the hell are you
looking at? Who do you think you are?"
—DAVID MCCULLOUGH, NARRATOR IN *SEABISCUIT*

• • •

When I play football, it's more controlled; at horse racing I'm an outsider. You just have to hope they go well, really.
—STEVE MCMANAMAN

• • •

Don't fall off.
—HOLLIE HUGHES, TO RON TURCOTTE,
SECRETARIAT'S JOCKEY, BEFORE THE 1973 BELMONT
STAKES

• • •

The skies were all blue as the bottom of a freshly painted pool. The white clapboard steeples of Churchill Downs, which had loomed over Thoroughbred races since the turn of the century, were brilliant in the sunshine.
—ELIZABETH MITCHELLE

• • •

If Carrie Ford wins the National I'll bare my backside to the wind and let everyone kick it.
—GINGER MCCAIN

• • •

A racetrack exists as a world apart, rich in its own mysteries and subject to laws of its own devising.
—BILL BARICH

• • •

The most famous race in the world is the Kentucky Derby, held on the first Saturday of May at Churchill Downs in Louisville at the distance of one-and-a-quarter miles.
—JOE DRAPE, *THE RACE FOR THE TRIPLE CROWN: HORSES, HIGH STAKES, AND ETERNAL HOPE*

• • •

I'm so shaken. It's just a gift from God.
—JOHN SERVIS'S WIFE SHERRY, AFTER SMARTY JONES WON THE SOUTHWEST STAKES

• • •

Of the more than six million horses in the United States, almost two million are used for showing. More than seven million people are involved in the horse industry and more than three and a half million are involved in showing.
—VICKY MOON

• • •

Racing in France is largely a silent ritual, played out for the benefit of a rich elite who have no particular interest in attracting the public to the track.
—ANDREW LONGMORE

• • •

I knew nothing about Standardbreds beyond the fact that they were long-bodied, harness-racing horses, sometimes called trotters because they raced at a trot.
—SUSAN RICHARDS, *CHOSEN BY A HORSE: A MEMOIR*

• • •

Horse races are short—two and a half minutes tops. They begin in mystery and probability. . . . A hundred and twenty seconds later, possibility will have metamorphosed into truth, fiction into fact, suspicion into realization.
—MAX WATMAN

• • •

I watched the race . . . but I only remember the last 200 yards, when the horses were charging past my seat. Flash Light took the lead and hurtled down the stretch like a running back headed for the end zone . . . this was the biggest thrill I'd had in months.
—TED MCCLELLAND, *HORSEPLAYERS*

• • •

If certainty about the past is so limited, must not certainty about the future be terribly slight? How can anybody wrench a profit from such confusion?
—TOM AINSLIE

• • •

No other sport is as profoundly affected by the start of a new year as Thoroughbred racing.
—T. D. THORNTON, *NOT BY A LONG SHOT*

• • •

If the horse is not familiar with its rider, or does not like that person, or if the rider is not attuned to the animal, the race can be lost during the post parade.
—TOM AINSLIE

• • •

In the sport of kings, Jerry Bailey is the king of kings.
—CHARLIE ROSE

• • •

I bought five more horses. Two are with the Canadian mounted
police. One's directing traffic out on Union Avenue. One is
up at Cornell; they can't figure out if it's a male or female.
And a last one a friend bought for $5,000 to spare me further
embarrassment.
—SAM RUBIN

• • •

Galloped because he was asked to gallop, because he knew it was
the right place for it. A great horse, with a great racing heart.
—DICK FRANCIS

• • •

There's always a moment in a race where a horse has to decide to
press on. A Thoroughbred is likelier than not to press on. That's
what we ask of them. But . . . at what cost? We rely on them . . .
to press on anyway. That's heart. . . . . . They have great hearts.
—JANE SMILEY, *HORSE HEAVEN*

• • •

To the rest of the country, the advance signs of spring are the
warble of birdies that sing. . . . But in the bluegrass country
of Kentucky, there is only one true harbinger of spring: the
Kentucky Derby.
—BERT SUGAR AND CORNELL RICHARDSON, *HORSE
SENSE: AN INSIDE LOOK AT THE SPORT OF KINGS*

• • •

Take one of those every half-mile and call me if there is any change.
—FROM *A DAY AT THE RACES*, MEDICAL ADVICE GIVEN TO A SICK RACE HORSE

• • •

With a gallantry that deserted him at the critical moment . . . his rider turned a somersault over his head and landed . . . sitting on the fence facing his horse's nose . . . he remained on the bank, towed the horse over, scrambled on to his back again and started afresh.
—SOMERVILLE AND ROSS

• • •

Ritual and routine are everything at the races. So to me, there is but one way to enter Suffolk Downs first thing in the morning— by a prescribed yet meandering route.
—T. D. THORNTON, *NOT BY A LONG SHOT*

• • •

Barclay Tagg was not exactly the sort that typically stands in the winner's circle smiling after the million-dollar race. Tagg is the kind of smart, hardworking reserved trainer that horsemen love.
—MAX WATMAN

• • •

If a horse has four legs, and I'm riding it, I think I can win.
—ANGEL CORDERO JR.

• • •

All that he remembers of the race at the turn was a jumble of colours, a kaleidoscope of horses and riders hanging on to the horses' necks.
—A. B. "BANJO" PATERSON

• • •

I was a racing fanatic . . . As a boy, I would drag the piano bench into my bedroom, fasten a Western riding saddle to it and envision myself in the greatest races of the day aboard any number of the greatest racehorses of the day.
—KY MORTENSEN

• • •

Man o' War, the Kentucky-bred who became a Kentucky legend, never raced in Kentucky—not in the Derby and not in any other race.
—THE BLOOD-HORSE STAFF, *THOROUGHBRED CHAMPIONS*

• • •

I may be romantic, but I do like to have ideals. I like to think that the average race is straight, and I believe it is. Maybe a race is straight because a horse is straight if he has a proper family tree. He's there to run because his kind have run. He's there to run because he's honest.
—J. P. MARQUAND

• • •

I'll be around as long as horses think I'm smarter than they are.
—JAMES E. "SUNNY JIM" FITZSIMMONS

• • •

A good jockey is one who settles his mount into a rhythm that even the most casual observer can notice. If a jockey is bouncing around on a horse like a pinball machine, then the horse has something else to think about other than running.
—C. N. RICHARDSON, *SMALL TRACK BETTING*

• • •

I never knew how to kiss rich people's asses, and I got too old to learn. If no owner was going to give me a big horse, I figured I'd have to find one myself.
—P. G. JOHNSON

• • •

A small red box with gold snap-lock and hinges sits atop a tall green safe. . . . It contains a triangular, three-sided, sterling silver vase approximately eight inches tall, which symbolizes the epitome of achievement for a three-year old Thoroughbred. It is the Triple Crown of American turfdom.
—MARVIN DRAGER, *THE MOST GLORIOUS CROWN*

• • •

You have to remember that about seventy percent of the horses running don't want to win. Horses are like people. Everybody doesn't have the aggressiveness or ambition to knock himself out to become a success.
—EDDIE ARCARO

• • •

Ask racing fans to name the greatest two horses of the twentieth century, and more times than not, you'll hear the names of Secretariat and Man o' War in either order. Though they raced more than fifty years apart, they are forever linked.
—BILL HELLER

• • •

The Kentucky Derby is a monument to him. It's his baby, and his alone. He will always be part of it, even more a part of it than the spired towers at Churchill Downs.
—ARTHUR DALEY, ON MATT WINN

• • •

That's a dam nice horse . . . you might depind your life on him.
—SOMERVILLE AND ROSS

• • •

I never met a Kentucky Derby I didn't like.
—JOE HIRSCH

• • •

Well, when I thought it over, I realized what that added up to. *We'd got the fastest horse in the world.* With the seven stone in the Cambridgeshire, 'e'd be like a racing car against push-bicycles.
—COLIN DAVEY

• • •

There just can't be anything smarter than a smart cutting horse. He can do everything but talk Meskin—and he understands that.
—JOE EVANS, *A CORRAL FULL OF STORIES*

• • •

chapter eight

"They Don't Call It Sitting": On Riding

Never take it for granted that this prey animal allows a predator to ride on his back. That's an amazing fact. You sit up there for one reason only—through his good grace.
—CRAIG CAMERON, *RIDE SMART*

• • •

It takes a bit of basic courage to ride beyond the status quo, but with each stride the view along that road becomes more and more exquisite.
—LESLIE DESMOND, *HORSE HANDLING AND RIDING THROUGH FEEL*

• • •

In order to have a saddle that is comfortable for the horse it has to be a little too big for the horse, especially at the front. This is because when a horse moves, his shoulder and back muscles have to bulge upwards. If a saddle fits snugly at rest it's actually too small when the horse starts to move.
—LINDA PARELLI

• • •

Unlike some of today's trendy methods (which rely on gimmicks, gadgets, or fatigue), dressage is rooted solidly in centuries of history: it was developed out of wartime maneuvers that required horses to respond calmly and instantly to a warrior's command—or face fatal consequences.
—LYNN PALM

• • •

It's the aspirin of horseback riding; it cures everything.
—NUNO OLIVERA, ON THE "SHOULDER-IN" DRESSAGE MOVEMENT

• • •

The first ten minutes of your ride [are] the "golden moments" where you show your horse your ability as a leader. And during that time, the only conversation you should have with the horse goes like this: "Hello. This is your Captain speaking!"
—JULIE GOODNIGHT

• • •

A saddle is something special just between you and your horse.
—STÜBBEN, SADDLE DEALERS

• • •

Holding our breath is something we all do when we're scared. But your breathing is noticeably copied by the horse, so good breathing is good first aid for releasing tensions in both of you in scary situations.
—GINCY SELF BUCKLIN, *MORE HOW YOUR HORSE WANTS YOU TO RIDE*

• • •

To err is human, but to blame the horse is even more human.
—PAT PARELLI

• • •

People who say they have no fear of horses are unsafe to be around.
—JOHN LYONS

• • •

A horse doesn't care how much you know until he knows how much you care.
—PAT PARELLI

• • •

There is a secret pleasing and cherishing of the horse with the bridle, which the rider must accomplish with so unperceiving a motion that none but the beast may know it.
—GERVAISE MARKHAM

• • •

I never encountered a horse in whose soul there was no harmony to call on.
—VICKI HEARNE

• • •

Anyone who has sat astride a horse will tell you that after their first time in the saddle, they found themselves incredibly sore and stiff. But any discomfort soon fades away, to be replaced by the joy of making new discoveries and experiencing revelations that are far more lasting.
—MOIRA C. HARRIS AND LIS CLEGG, *RIDING*

• • •

They don't call it sitting, they call it riding.
—CRAIG CAMERON, *RIDE SMART*

• • •

Personally, the only horse who I ever set on their back throwed me off on my bosom before I had road him twenty feet and did the horse wait to see if I was hurt, no.
—RING LARDNER, *TIPS ON HORSES*

• • •

In riding these wild, vicious horses . . . especially at night, accidents are always occurring. A man who is merely an ordinary rider is certain to have a pretty hard time.
—THEODORE ROOSEVELT

• • •

Horses see in black and white, and riders ride in grey.
—CINDY ISHOY

• • •

Developing a dependable source of remounts has plagued man ever since he began to ride horseback thousands of years ago. As a hunter and warrior, he was only as good as the horse under him.
—PHIL LIVINGSTON AND ED ROBERTS, *WAR HORSE: MOUNTING THE CAVALRY WITH AMERICA'S FINEST HORSES*

• • •

No one ever promised that the fastest horse in the race was the easiest one to ride.
—ERIC J. JOINER JR.

• • •

All that I could do in a race was to sit still and try to stay on, and that this was exactly the sort of rider the old horse needed to get the best out of him.
—JOHN WELCOME, *A GLASS OF PORT WITH THE PROCTOR*

• • •

Always smile when you are riding because it changes your intent.
—JAMES SHAW

• • •

Riders . . . know in their head what they did wrong. . . . If you allow yourself to make excuses, you're not going to get better.
—STEVE ASMUSSEN

• • •

When one is on horseback he knows all things.
—GEORGE HERBERT

• • •

Riding teaches him self-esteem and control of himself and of something else—this animal.
—GENE SMITH, *THE CHAMPION*

• • •

When riding a horse we leave our fear, troubles, and sadness behind on the ground.
—JULIE CARLSON

• • •

Did you come to hide or did you come to ride?
—PAUL ZARZYSKI, *GOOD HORSE KEEPING*

• • •

A horse which stops dead just before a jump and thus propels its rider into a graceful arc provides a splendid excuse for general merriment.
—PRINCE PHILIP, DUKE OF EDINBURGH

• • •

When life hands me lemons, I don't make lemonade, I go for a ride; horses are my family.
—JUDY RICHTER

• • •

It lies in the hands of every single rider whether horse and rider feel relaxed. It must be every rider's supreme aim to create relaxation of mind and body.
—KLAUS BALKENHOL

• • •

There are no problem horses—only problem riders.
—MARY TWELVEPONIES

• • •

Horses had never scared him because he had been born to the saddle and had grown up mastering everything on four legs with contemptuous ease. He believed in his heart that no one could really ride better than he could.
—DICK FRANCIS, *A CARROT FOR A CHESTNUT*

• • •

And the horse was never saddled that the Geebungs couldn't ride.
—A. B. (BANJO) PATERSON, *THE GEEBUNG POLO CLUB*

• • •

Never a pony couldn't be rode, never a cowboy couldn't be throwed.
—PAUL ZARZYSKI, *GOOD HORSE KEEPING*

• • •

I ride because I rode as a child when life was simpler and somehow more complete.
—M. ADELIA RAMEY, *ALWAYS THERE ARE HORSES*

• • •

Had I but known about breathing in my youth, how much simpler my competitive riding life would have been.
—VICTOR HUGO-VIDAL

• • •

Before you swing a leg over a horse, you should know why you're swinging it.
—MARLENE MCRAE, *BARREL RACING 101: A COMPLETE PROGRAM FOR HORSE AND RIDER*

• • •

Riding is a partnership. The horse lends you his strength, speed and grace, which are greater than yours. For your part, you give him your guidance, intelligence, and understanding, which are greater than his. Together, you can achieve a richness that alone neither can.
—LUCY REES, *THE HORSE'S MIND*

• • •

He rode a splendid horse that was born for a racer and fed and lodged like a gentleman; kept him at his utmost speed for ten miles, and then . . . the transfer of rider and mail-bag was made in the twinkling of an eye.
—MARK TWAIN

• • •

Get pitched off, climb right back on.
—PAUL ZARZYSKI, *GOOD HORSE KEEPING*

• • •

There is nothing in which a horse's power is better revealed than in a neat, clean stop.
—MICHEL DE MONTAIGNE

• • •

The horse and rider are elemental. They ride at the heart of the wind of God.
—J. PHILIP NEWELL

• • •

There is something about riding down the street on a prancing horse that makes you feel like something, even when you ain't a thing.
—WILL ROGERS

• • •

A horse's eye disquiets me: it has an expression of alarm that may at any moment be translated into action.
—E. V. LUCAS

• • •

We have almost forgotten how strange a thing it is that so huge and powerful and intelligent an animal as a horse should allow another, and far more feeble animal, to ride upon its back.
—PETER GRAY

• • •

Speak your mind, but ride a fast horse.
—ANONYMOUS

• • •

She had ridden with Grey Horse before she could walk, held firmly in his arms as he cantered back and forth from the herd. By the age of ten, she was constantly riding at his side from camp to camp.
—TYLER TAFFORD, *THE STORY OF BLUE EYE*

• • •

You'll never know how much you love to be on a horse . . . until you fall off!
—ANONYMOUS

• • •

Many riding accidents would never have happened if people could control the false pride that makes them almost ashamed to ask for a quiet horse.
—GORDON WRIGHT, *LEARNING TO RIDE, HUNT, AND SHOW*

• • •

This is the time I ride Colonel every day. I told you how he waits for me. He knows the time.
—ANN RINALDI, *A RIDE INTO MORNING: THE STORY OF TEMPE WICK*

• • •

When you are on a great horse, you have the best seat you will ever have.
—SIR WINSTON CHURCHILL

• • •

In riding a horse we borrow freedom.
—HELEN THOMSON

• • •

To ride a horse well, you have to know it as well as you know your best friend.
—KATIE MONAHAN PRUDENT

• • •

Do in *your* body what you want your horse to do in *his*. That's the whole simple secret to riding with fluidity.
—LINDA PARELLI

• • •

I've spent most of my life riding horses. The rest I've just wasted.
—ANONYMOUS

• • •

Her gaits were so smooth that I felt like we were flying. She seemed able to do whatever I asked, responding with enthusiasm and a little extra spunk.
—CHRISTA IACONO, *THE PERFECT HORSE*

• • •

A horse's behavior will be in direct proportion to the number of people watching you ride him.
—COOKY MCCLUNG

• • •

It felt as though she unfurled an invisible sail between strides, so that when her feet were off the ground she rode the wind at her back.
—YATES KENNEDY, ON RUFFIAN

• • •

Once a rider has found trust in his horse's abilities, he can develop the confidence needed to achieve special accomplishments.
—ELIZABETH FURST

• • •

The rider of a responsive Western horse must anticipate and lead the horse with a weight-shift cue. If in turning to the right, the rider turns her body and looks to the right, she leads the horse, and the responsive horse moves under the rider's weight, bringing them back into balance.
—DON BLAZER, *NATURAL WESTERN RIDING*

• • •

A good rider can hear his horse speak to him. A great rider can hear his horse whisper.
—ANONYMOUS

• • •

I want my horse to look and feel his best.
—MARLENE MCRAE, *BARREL RACING 101: A COMPLETE PROGRAM FOR HORSE AND RIDER*

• • •

To expect to ride without encountering difficulties and worries, as well as risks and dangers, is only to look for something that cannot possibly be attained.
—*RIDING FOR LADIES*, 1887

• • •

Spoiled horses, difficult horses, and even rogues, can teach us much that is important; the rider who is too well mounted may never really learn to ride.
—WILLIAM C. STEINKRAUS, *RIDING AND JUMPING*

• • •

"They Don't Call It Sitting": On Riding

Feeling down? Saddle up. It is the only cure.
—ANONYMOUS

• • •

Don't be the rider who gallops all night and never sees the horse
that is beneath him
—RUMI (1207–1273)

• • •

If the horse does not enjoy his work, his rider will have no joy.
—H. H. ISENBART

• • •

We shall take great care not to annoy the horse and spoil his
friendly charm, for it is like the scent of a blossom—once lost it
will never return.
—ANTOINE DE PLUVINEL (1552–1620)

• • •

[The mare] set off for home with the speed of a swallow, and
going as smoothly and silently. I never had dreamed of such a
motion, fluent and graceful, and ambient, soft as the breeze flit-
ting over the flowers, but swift as the summer lightning.
—RICHARD DODDRIDGE BLACKMORE (1825–1900)

• • •

Riding: The art of keeping a horse between you and the ground.
—ANONYMOUS

• • •

Ride the horse in the direction that it's going.
—WERNER ERHARD

• • •

It is not enough for a man to know how to ride; he must know how to fall.
—MEXICAN PROVERB

• • •

Horses are uncomfortable in the middle and dangerous at both ends.
—ATTRIBUTED TO VARIOUS

• • •

Most persons do not ride; they are conveyed.
—M. F. MCTAGGART

• • •

I never mount a horse without experiencing a sort of dread that I may be setting out on that last mysterious journey which all of us must take sooner or later, and I never come back in safety from a horseback trip without thinking of my latter end for two or three days afterward.
—MARK TWAIN

• • •

When pride rideth in the saddle, destruction rideth on the crupper.
—ANONYMOUS

• • •

"They Don't Call It Sitting": On Riding

It is a disease for which there is no cure. You will go on riding
even after they have to haul you on a comfortable wise old cob,
with feet like inverted buckets and a back like a fireside chair.
—MONICA DICKENS (1915–1992)

• • •

"Well, suh, about the head of a truly great hawse there is an air
of freedom unconquerable. The eyes seem to look on heights
beyond our gaze. It is the look of the spirit that can soar."
—JOHN TAINTOR FOOTE, *THE LOOK OF EAGLES*

• • •

The chestnut horse galloped through sun and wind, stars and
snow, looking for a place where there was no Death.
—SALLY POMME CLAYTON, *TALES TOLD IN TENTS:
STORIES FROM CENTRAL ASIA*

• • •

When I rode for myself, that's when I got better. It's a matter of
confidence and getting used to showing.
—LINDA ZANG

• • •

The worst part is over,
Now, get back on that horse and ride.
—JAMES MERCER OF THE SHINS, "TURN ON ME"

• • •

A canter is a cure for every evil.
—BENJAMIN DISRAELI

• • •

At its finest, rider and horse are joined not by tack, but by trust. Each is totally reliant upon the other. Each is the selfless guardian of the other's well-being.
—ANONYMOUS

• • •

Men are better when riding, more just and more understanding, and more alert and more at ease and more under-taking, and better knowing of all countries and all passages; in short and long all good customs and manners cometh thereof, and the health of man and of his soul.
—ATTRIBUTED TO VARIOUS

• • •

Ridin' for the brand is an often misunderstood concept in that it requires an obligation from both parties.
—WADDIE MITCHELL

• • •

Being with my horses gives me a sense of inner calm and satisfaction that I can carry with me. It improves my ability to handle the stresses of my job and gives me a wonderful perspective on life.
—SPRING SWINEHART

• • •

The stopping of a horse dramatically so that it would not move. That was called . . . *jading* a horse; and . . . the horsemen sometimes earned the name of *horse-witches* because they were able to make the horse stand as though it were paralyzed or bewitched.
—ANTHONY DENT, *THE HORSE THROUGH FIFTY CENTURIES OF CIVILIZATION*

• • •

There is something about jumping a horse over a fence, something that makes you feel good. Perhaps it's the risk, the gamble. In any event it's a thing I need.
—WILLIAM FAULKNER

• • •

There is nothing like a rattling ride for curing melancholy!
—WINTHROP MACKWORTH PRAED (1802–1839)

• • •

Listen to the horses clipping, clopping,
hoofbeats everywhere never stopping. . . .
—RAFFI

• • •

When riding a high-strung horse, pretend you are riding an old one.
—DOMINIQUE BARBIER

• • •

He bows his nose to his chest and prances, his tail lifted proudly and he cocks his head toward me as he passes. I'm smitten and he knows it.
—MERRI MELDE, *FOR THE LOVE OF RACEHORSES*

• • •

Riding becomes a break from reality, a time when I know why I am.
—GAWANI PONY BOY, *OF WOMEN AND HORSES*

• • •

The rhythm of the ride carried them on and on, and she knew that the horse was as eager as she, as much in love with the speed and air and freedom.
—GEORGESS MCHARGUE

• • •

"I'd rather ride for the devil himself," said he, "than ride a horse for Cousin Honour."
—MOLLY KEANE

• • •

There's a variety of horse minds as big as there is among human minds. Some need more persuading than others, and a few of 'em, no matter how firm they're handled, will have to be showed again and again that they can't get away with this or that.
—WILL JAMES, *SMOKY THE COWHORSE*

• • •

The sport of show jumping turns a glamorous face to the world.
—NANCY JAFFER

• • •

In a second or two it becomes a horse and rider, rising and falling, rising and falling—sweeping towards us nearer and nearer—growing more and more distinct, more and more sharply defined—nearer and still nearer, and the flutter of the hoofs comes faintly to the ear . . .
—MARK TWAIN, *ROUGHING IT*

• • •

I think jumping is the biggest thrill of all. It's the closest thing to flying. Nothing feels better than galloping down a big jump and having a horse take flight. It's like being superhuman.
—NONA GARSON

• • •

The horse you get off is not the same as the horse you got on. It is your job as a rider to ensure that as often as possible, the change is for the better.
—CORMAC MCCARTHY, *CITIES OF THE PLAIN*

• • •

No ride is ever the last one. No horse is ever the last one you will have. Somehow there will always be other horses, other places to ride them.
—MONICA DICKENS

• • •

On the worst day, I think I have the best job in the world.
—NONA GARSON, ON SHOW JUMPING

• • •

Riders who force their horses by the use of the whip only increase their fear for they then associate the pain with the thing that frightens them.
—XENOPHON

• • •

May your horse never stumble.
—SALLY POMME CLAYTON, *TALES TOLD IN TENTS: STORIES FROM CENTRAL ASIA*

• • •

Women who ride, as a rule, ride better than men. They, the women, have always been instructed; whereas men usually come to ride without any instruction.
—ANTHONY TROLLOPE, *THE LADY WHO RIDES TO HOUNDS*

• • •

Sing, riding's a joy!
For me I ride.
—ROBERT BROWNING, *THE LAST RIDE TOGETHER*

• • •

I ride because of all the horses I shall never ride.
—M. ADELIA RAMEY

• • •

Fear almost always arises—in horses as well as in people—from concern about what might happen, and much more rarely from what *is* happening.
—MARY WANLESS

• • •

The way a person sits on a horse is exactly the way a mountain lion would . . . it's easy to understand why a horse wouldn't be that interested in a person crawling up on top of him like some would-be mountain lion clamping down his feet!
—BUCK BRANNAMAN

• • •

He who would ride a horse must learn to fall.
—SPANISH PROVERB

• • •

Equestrian art, however, is something else which involves complete harmony between horse and rider, and that makes the rider feel that there have been moments of beauty and greatness which make a flight possible from all that is ordinary and mediocre.
—NUNO OLIVEIRA

• • •

I add riding to my list of things that look easier than they are!
—MELISSA SOVEY-NELSON, *IF I HAD A HORSE*

• • •

There are times when you can trust a horse, times when you can't, and times when you have to.
—ANONYMOUS

• • •

He soared over every fence as if he had wings.
—STEPHEN BUDIANSKY, *TALLYHO AND TRIBULATION*

• • •

He wheeled the cart up to him, got him harnessed to it, and in two minutes that pony was walking, trotting, anything I wanted—can't explain why—one of the mysteries of horseflesh.
—SOMERVILLE AND ROSS

• • •

I, who travel most often for my pleasure, do not direct myself so badly. If it looks ugly on the right, I take the left; if I find myself unfit to ride my horse, I stop. . . . Have I left something unseen behind me? I go back; it is still on my road. I trace no fixed line, either straight or crooked.
—MICHEL DE MONTAIGNE

• • •

I sit astride life like a bad rider on a horse. I only owe it to the horse's good nature that I am not thrown off at this very moment.
—LUDWIG WITTGENSTEIN (1889–1951)

• • •

Half the failures of this world arise from pulling in one's horse as he is leaping.
—JULIUS HARE (1795–1855), *GUESSES AT TRUTH*

• • •

Equitation is not the search for public acclaim and self satisfaction after applause. Nor is it the pleasure of every prize or a judge or jury's admiration at a show. It is the head-to-head dialogue with the horse and the search for communication and perfection.
—NUNO OLIVEIRA

• • •

Henry Miller once said that a hero is a man who has conquered his fears. . . . I began to be a heroine when I sat on the back of a horse for the first time . . .
—INGRID SOREN, *ZEN AND HORSES*

• • •

Lord Ronald said nothing; he flung himself from the room, flung himself upon his horse and rode madly off in all directions.
—STEPHEN LEACOCK, *GERTRUDE THE GOVERNESS*

• • •

[T]he lad with the ankle-length boots and spurs two inches long and his breeches worn over his stockings, riding a savage of a brown horse that had killed one man and frightened several so badly that they never wanted to ride again.
—MOLLY KEANE, *PRIME ROGUES*

• • •

Green on green makes black and blue.
—TRADITIONAL CAUTION ABOUT WHAT HAPPENS WHEN A GREEN OR NOVICE RIDER RIDES A GREEN HORSE

• • •

Love, not force, rides the horse.
—SAIOM SHRIVER

• • •

Those who love horses are impelled by an ever-receding vision, some enchanted transformation through which the horse and the rider become a third, much greater thing.
—THOMAS MCGUANE

• • •

If the horses knew their strength we should not ride anymore.
—MARK TWAIN

• • •

Each handicap is like a hurdle in a steeplechase, and when you ride up to it, if you throw your heart over, the horse will go along too.
—LAWRENCE BIXBY

• • •

It seems no coincidence . . . that the history of our country is bound up with that of the horse; the very act of riding continuing the chronicle of horsemen and horsewomen who have left their marks on history from the saddle in years past.
—DONNA SNYDER-SMITH, *THE ALL-AROUND HORSE AND RIDER*

• • •

Riding preserves during the physical development a precise balance between strength and suppleness. This special quality, which naturally involves moral values too, leads to more balanced and disciplined training. Thus riding—the complete sport *par excellence*—tempers the body as it does the spirit.
—COMMANDANT JEAN LICART

• • •

The horse never knows I'm there until he needs me.
—WILLIE SHOEMAKER

• • •

So sudden is it all, and so like the flash of unreal fancy . . . we might have doubted whether we had seen any actual horse and man at all, maybe.
—MARK TWAIN

• • •

A man in passion rides a horse that runs away with him.
—THOMAS FULLER

• • •

Think of riding as a science, but love it as an art.
—GEORGE MORRIS

• • •

It was on horseback that man would first experience the exhilaration of the whipping wind and the flashing landscape.
—FULVIO CINQUINI, *MAN AND HORSE: AN ENDURING BOND*

• • •

Find your horse. Discover the direction the horse is going. Ride the horse in that direction.
—PETER MCWILLIAMS

• • •

I had lived with horses all my life. I seemed to be constitutionally incapable of sitting on one over a fence. This happens to a few unlucky people and I was one of them.
—JOHN WELCOME

• • •

Good riders constantly improve their riding skills.
—CHARMAYNE JAMES, *CHARMAYNE JAMES ON BARREL RACING*

• • •

My early riding days were spent on the wooden, or rocking variety of mount. Armchairs, bedsteads, all served in my apprenticeship—in fact, my parents' furniture still bears the mark of my whip and improvised spurs!
—ALAN OLIVER

• • •

Never ride your horse more than five-and-thirty miles a day, always taking more care of him than of yourself; which is right and reasonable, seeing as how the horse is the best animal of the two.
—GEORGE BORROW (1803–1881)

• • •

No horse gets anywhere until he is harnessed.
—HARRY EMERSON FOSDICK

• • •

I have seven horses. I'm known to go off on my horse for about six hours in the wilderness.
—ARMAND ASSANTE

• • •

The rhythm of the ride carried them on and on, and she knew that the horse was as eager as she, as much in love with the speed and air and freedom.
—GEORGESS MCHARGUE

• • •

The horse provides the locomotor energy, and the rider has the prerogative of determining the goal and of guiding the movements of his powerful mount towards it. But all too often . . . the rider is obliged to guide his horse in the direction in which it itself wants to go.
—SIGMUND FREUD

• • •

Listen to its hooves hitting the ground, a living drum. Each hoofbeat resounds in a four-beat quatrain, the rhythm many great poets use to turn words into music.
—ADELE MCCORMICK AND MARLENA MCCORMICK, *HORSE SENSE AND THE HUMAN HEART*

• • •

I ride my horse at competition level.
—ALANNAH MYLES

• • •

Awareness takes you beyond the mechanics of your riding.
—JILL KEISER HASSLER, *BEYOND THE MIRRORS*

• • •

A catcher and his body are like the outlaw and his horse. He's got to ride that nag till it drops.
—JOHNNY BENCH

And he will ride this year! He is fixed to that purpose. He will ride straight—and, if possible, he will like it.
—ANTHONY TROLLOPE

• • •

If you're riding a horse and it dies, get off . . .
—JIM GRANT AND CHAR FORSTEN

• • •

Every time you ride, you're either teaching or un-teaching your horse.
—GORDON WRIGHT

• • •

They rode with great speed; and both men and horses were covered with dust and blood.
—JAMES BALDWIN (1924–1987)

• • •

A man who rode good horses was usually a good man.
—WESTERN EXPRESSION

• • •

Horses can be scary animals to work with, due to their size and apparent skittishness, but often fear of an animal is just covering up other personal issues that the person is trying to deal with.
—BUCK BRANNAMAN

• • •

There are few things more exciting than releasing a band of young horses from a corral where they have been confined for some time into open space and watching the explosion of movement as these meteors take an open country.
—THOMAS MCGUANE

• • •

It is also well known that good horses bring happiness to the heart of the riders, if they are at least reasonably skilled.
—EDWARD OF PORTUGAL (1391–1438)

• • •

When riding a horse we leave our fear, troubles, and sadness behind on the ground.
—JULIE CARLSON

• • •

If anybody expects to calm a horse down by tiring him out with riding swiftly and far, his supposition is the reverse of the truth.
—XENOPHON

• • •

169

Women who have had the same opportunities as men of learning to ride, ride quite well. . . . But as a rule they do not *get* the chance of excelling, not are they "set right" by unpalatable home truths being told them without favor or affection.
—ALICE HAYES, *THE HORSEWOMAN*

• • •

Riding is simple . . . it's just not easy.
—ANONYMOUS

• • •

Just sit back. If you lie back you'll only be upright to the ground. Don't jerk his head whatever you do. It's a long way down but he'll land steady. Just keep him as still as if you were a dummy, and put confidence into him.
—ENID BAGNOLD

• • •

To judge a horse by its rider, is to judge a book by its cover.
—ANONYMOUS

• • •

No gymnastics could be better or harder exercise, and this and the art of riding, are of all the arts the most befitting a free man.
—PLATO

• • •

Most persons do not ride; they are conveyed.
—M. F. MCTAGGART

• • •

The quality of the jump is determined by the quality of the approach to the fence, which is itself determined by the quality of the getaway from the previous fence and the turns between the two jumps.
—MARY WANLESS, *THE NATURAL RIDER*

• • •

Whenever difficulties appear, the rider must ask himself: does the horse not want to execute my demands, does he not understand what I want, or is he physically unable to carry them out? The rider's conscience must find the answer.
—ALOIS PODHAJSKY (1898–1973)

• • •

As a good horse is not very apt to jump over a bank, if left to guide himself, I let mine pick his own way.
—BUFFALO BILL

• • •

There are two important rules in horse-riding. The first is to mount the horse. The second is to stay mounted.
—ANONYMOUS

• • •

The horse thinks one thing and he who saddles him another.
—ATTRIBUTED TO VARIOUS

• • •

chapter nine

Horse Sense: On Training, Taming, Schooling, Breaking, Gentling, and the Like

One man's correct lead is another man's counter-canter.
—STEVE PRICE

• • •

Most conventionally started horses form an adversarial relationship with the humans who employ them. If they agree to perform, it is with a reluctant attitude. The first rule of starting a fresh horse, then, is *no pain.*
—MONTY ROBERTS

• • •

We can do little to teach the horse; we can only create an environment in which he can learn.
—MONTY ROBERTS

• • •

If a horse is capable of doing what you ask, it is up to you to ask in such a way that he will do it. Once you understand that the answer to your horse's problems is in finding your own mistakes, you are on your way to finding the correct solutions.
—MARY TWELVEPONIES

• • •

A lot of people get along pretty well with their horses until they go to training those horses.
—TOM DORRANCE, *TRUE UNITY: WILLING COMMUNICATION BETWEEN HORSE AND RIDER*

• • •

Now I submit that the first thing a man who owns a horse should obtain is knowledge of the foot and the best method of protecting it [. . .]. A horse without sound feet is no horse at all.
—W. H. MURRAY

• • •

The horse is a natural-born skeptic. He's a coward at heart. He's claustrophobic, and boy, when things get too close, too tight, he becomes a full-throttle-aholic. Instantly! He doesn't think. He reacts.
—RONNIE WILLIS

• • •

I do believe that things like education by and large serve to defraud humans of their own interests and sometimes thereby of their souls, and that crazy horses are one consequence of the "education" of horses.
—VICKI HEARNE, *ADAM'S TASK*

• • •

I have often noticed that good horsemen are like good sailors, meticulously and quietly tending to one detail after another, all to keep things running smoothly and safely.
—TOM MCGUANE

• • •

Work on your horse by working on yourself.
—TOM DORRANCE

• • •

They say that a person hasn't really learned a foreign language until he has learned to think in it. The same thing applies to training a horse. When he has learned to think in your language, then he is really trained.
—MARY TWELVEPONIES

• • •

If you're going to teach a horse something and have a good relationship, you don't make him learn it—you let him learn it.
—RAY HUNT

• • •

The better your horse backs up and goes sideways, the better he does everything else.
—PAT PARELLI

• • •

175

Remember that an easy hand is one of the principal aids we have; for it puts a horse upon its haunches, when he finds nothing else to learn upon; it pleases him, and prevents his being resty.
—WILLIAM CAVENDISH

• • •

The worst kick is from a trained horse.
—CORSICAN PROVERB

• • •

Our indirect methods have taught us a mountain of things about horses, but if you wished to learn even more, would you rather be Whirlaway in the stretch, than interview Eddie Arcaro afterwards?
—STEPHEN JAY GOULD

• • •

When the spring round-up begins the horses should be as fat and sleek as possible. After running all winter free, even the most sober pony is apt to betray an inclination to buck; and, if possible, we like to ride every animal once or twice before we begin to do real work with him.
—THEODORE ROOSEVELT

• • •

[Horse] gentlers talk, not about people with horse problems, but horses with people problems. About the horse as teacher, about the slow way with horses as the quickest way. This is a horse-centered worldview that gentlers say offers a nice spinoff: It makes humans more humane.
—LAWRENCE SCANLAN

• • •

The educated horse is a thinking horse, and it seems that he understands that every now and then something happens that he must chalk up as a mistake and be done with it.
—DENNIS MURPHY

• • •

What you know for certain is that you don't know nothing for certain.
—ALLEN JERKENS

• • •

It was clear right away that horses had personalities and moods. Some became my friends and some stayed enemies until the day I left. Most interesting of all: They seemed more afraid of me than I was of them.
—CHRIS IRWIN, *HORSES DON'T LIE*

• • •

The school horse is a very important, almost indispensable assistant to the instructor. But he will be of full value only if the instructor is thoroughly acquainted with his movements and his temperament.
—ALOIS PODHAJSKY, *MY HORSES, MY TEACHERS*

• • •

You took care of your horse, and your horse took care of you.
—ELTON GALLEGLY

• • •

[H]e is not seeking companionship with horses, though his relationship with horses he likes . . . is equivalent to the consistent respect one accords an esteemed co-worker.
—THOMAS MCGUANE

• • •

177

A good grooming is equivalent to half a feed.
—CAPTAIN DE CONDENBOVE, FRENCH ARMY,
WORLD WAR I. THIS APPEARED IN *FIELD ARTILLERY
MANUAL, VOL. 1*, BY ARTHUR R. WILSON, CAPT.,
FIELD ARTILLERY, U.S. ARMY, 1926

• • •

There is no doubt that horse work was the roughest and most
arduous part of our life.
—JAMES HERRIOT, *ALL THINGS BRIGHT AND
BEAUTIFUL*

• • •

Positive horse training . . . defines the horse-human relationship
as a team, with reasonable motivations and logical rewards for
cooperation. Positive horse training uses well-timed rewards to
build trust and respect between horse and human.
—SARAH BLANCHARD, *THE POWER OF POSITIVE
HORSE TRAINING*

• • •

The books say never lead a Thoroughbred without that chain
over his nose so you can pull him down sharply and really rap
him, and I have heard Louise Meryman . . . tell her students
they should never even lead a Thoroughbred across a courtyard
without a metal chain on his nose.
—GENE SMITH, *THE CHAMPION*

• • •

The novice may want a trainer to work with a horse to correct deficiencies in its training or to help improve the novice's equitation or to prevent gross mistakes in training or riding.
—J. WARREN EVANS

• • •

A real horseman must not only be an expert—he must also be able to think and feel like a horse, that is, to realize that a horse is not equipped with human understanding.
—WALDEMAR SEUNIG

• • •

For, everything that we get [a horse] to do of his own accord, without force, must be accomplished by some means of conveying our ideas to his mind.
—JOHN RAREY (1827–1866)

• • •

[T]he horse has one factor which a machine does not have; it has a brain. Not a very large one, it is true, but large enough to introduce a random element of uncertainty into its operation.
—JACK COGGINS, *THE HORSEMAN'S BIBLE*

• • •

It can be set down in four words: the best of everything. The best hay, oats, and water.
—JAMES E. "SUNNY JIM" FITZSIMMONS

• • •

It is also good to pet the beast while he eats so that he will relax.
—MARCUS AURELIUS

• • •

No instructor is capable of teaching this delicate language between rider and horse without the willing assistance of the horse.
—ALOIS PODHAJSKY

• • •

The first and most important basic is a good attitude toward the horse. I know that many of us were taught that we must "master" the horse. . . . I do feel that his kind of thinking is . . . outdated.
—GINCY SELF BUCKLIN, *HOW YOUR HORSE WANTS YOU TO RIDE*

• • •

A horse cannot be expected to understand exactly what you want it to do the first time it is asked. It will, however, know when it has done something right if you will show that you are pleased.
—COLIN VOGEL, *COMPLETE HORSE CARE MANUAL*

• • •

If a horse is no good, sell him for a dog.
—BEN JONES

• • •

When a horse is galloping, each leg in turn supports his entire weight.
—PRESTON M. BURCH AND ALEX BOWER, *TRAINING THOROUGHBRED HORSES*

• • •

He is my silent teacher . . . guiding me to understanding.
—CAROLE HUDGENS

• • •

Horses are really high-maintenance creatures, and goats are low-maintenance creatures. I'm sorry I can't ride my goats, but I still love them just the same. I wish I had time for horses.
—KRIST NOVOSELIC

• • •

Horses are the same from the day they're born to the day they die. They are only changed by the people who train them.
—TOM SMITH

• • •

The greatest error in training horses lies in not showing up for work often enough and trying to accomplish too much when you do.
—TOM MCGUANE

• • •

If you have a problem getting along with neighbors or people in school, you might as well forget about training horses. Training horses is not fighting with them. And it's not a business for a person who is lazy. It takes a lot of drive.
—MARVIN MAYFIELD

• • •

The young rider, eager to learn, may rely on his four-legged teacher whose importance sometimes even rises above that of the two-legged one.
—ALOIS PODHAJSKY

• • •

The majority of horses are willing and anxious to please and will
give a great deal in exchange for a little praise and
kind treatment.
—JACK COGGINS, *THE HORSEMAN'S BIBLE*

• • •

The shoulder-in is the aspirin of equitation; it cures everything.
—NUNO OLIVEIRA

• • •

Pet me sometimes, be always gentle to me so that I may serve you
more gladly and learn to love you.
—CAPTAIN DE CONDENBOVE, FRENCH ARMY,
WORLD WAR I. THIS APPEARED IN *FIELD ARTILLERY
MANUAL, VOL. 1*, BY ARTHUR R. WILSON, CAPT.,
FIELD ARTILLERY, U.S. ARMY, 1926

• • •

That moment of complete mutual respect and trust marks the
beginning of a relationship between a horse and human that's
one of the most special relationships you can have with an
animal.
—BUCK BRANNAMAN

• • •

For me it is first and last about the relationship between a human being and a horse, nothing more. If a person . . . strives for integrity, humanity, truth and inner awareness and if he is prepared to question himself . . . it is . . . enough for the horses, because they seek mutuality, not differences.
—KLAUS FERDINAND HEMPFLING, *WHAT HORSES REVEAL: FROM FIRST ENCOUNTER TO FRIEND FOR LIFE*

• • •

Since the horse cannot speak the rider must endeavor to guess his thoughts and to interpret his reactions and draw conclusions from his behavior.
—ALOIS PODHAJSKY

• • •

I do know that I fell off just about every one of them. Even if I was hurt, as happened a couple of times, my father would always make me get right back on and ride some more.
—CAREY WINFREY

• • •

In its strict meaning, "dressage" is simply the training of the horse. In use, though, dressage has become the art and intensely competitive sport of training in the classical movements. Like figure skating, dressage emphasizes the power and beauty of motion. . . .
—HOLLY MENINO, *THE PONIES ARE TALKING*

• • •

To properly train your horse, you have to be very patient.
—TWILA DIAN, *ALL ABOUT HORSES*

• • •

The secret to success with horses is knowledge, consistency, and time. You get consistency from understanding, which comes from knowledge—and you have to put in the time.
—STACY WESTFALL

• • •

A horse can be made to do almost anything if his master has intelligence enough to let him know what is required.
—ULYSSES S. GRANT (1822–1885)

• • •

It's what you learn after you know it all that's important.
—JIMMY WILLIAMS

• • •

I have a new horse. I get her to come to me from half a mile away. With just a simple call. That's because she knows that when she's with me, she's taken care of. She trusts me.
—RUSSELL CROWE

• • •

There are many types of bits for many different disciplines, but the severity of all bits lies in the hands holding them.
—MONTY ROBERTS

• • •

If training has not made a horse more beautiful, nobler in carriage, more attentive in his behavior, revealing pleasure in his own accomplishment . . . then he has not truly been schooled in dressage.
—COLONEL HANS HANDLER

• • •

No time spent in the saddle is wasted; as you learn to communicate with the horse and appreciate what he can do for you, it will add a fascinating dimension to your life.
—MARY GORDON-WATSON, *THE HANDBOOK OF RIDING*

• • •

Horses are not really intelligent; but they learn quickly . . . they learn what humans consider bad behavior just as easily as good behavior if they are allowed to. You must be careful not to allow a horse to learn that it can get what it wanted through undesirable behavior.
—COLIN VOGEL, *COMPLETE HORSE CARE MANUAL*

• • •

The way you start a colt is critical. Once [Tom Dorrance] taught us to be softer, kinder, gentler, our horses worked better. It actually makes a difference when a horse likes you.
—GREG WARD

• • •

Horses are much more adept at recognizing fear than we humans.
—KELLY MARKS

• • •

A rider's total belief in an instructor is . . . essential.
—GEORGE H. MORRIS

• • •

One longtime observer of horse sports remarked to me that a dressage rider could look at the horse standing in his stall and instantly detect a new fly bite on the animal.
—HOLLY MENINO, *THE PONIES ARE TALKING*

• • •

The art of horsemanship assumes many forms . . .
—CHARLENE STRICKLAND, *WESTERN PRACTICE LESSONS*

• • •

A ruthlessly condensed training only leads to a general superficiality, to travesties of the movements, and to a premature unsoundness of the horse. Nature cannot be violated.
—ALOIS PODHAJSKY

• • •

You need to get inside their head and understand them. If you use force on animals bred for hundreds of years to be war horses, they will wage war with you. You can't own them. You can befriend them. Loving these horses—if it's in your heart, you will never lose the passion.
—CHEN KEDAR

• • •

A true horseman demands respect from horses because he or she knows it's critical for safety. He or she also respects the horse: his size, instincts, and character. When you both feel safe and have mutual respect, you develop trust and confidence.
—BOB AVILA

• • •

Never . . . telegraph to your horse how you feel unless you want him to feel the same. No creature is more sensitive to mood than a horse. He will at once recognize fear or impatience on the part of his rider.
—MACGREGOR JENKINS

• • •

The horse does not execute down transitions by pulling the fore-hand backwards, but by stepping under his hind legs.
—E. F. SEDLER

• • •

As a general rule ponies are considerably more intelligent than horses, are less easily frightened, and seldom panic. Their more phlegmatic disposition also enables them to tolerate the rough-housing and the excess of petting and attention which kids enjoy so much.
—JACK COGGINS, *THE HORSEMAN'S BIBLE*

• • •

Dressage, the art for art's sake school of horsemanship, does not involve the speed or danger of other horse sports, but many top riders have left fast times and big fences for the intellectual stimulation of manège and the rigor of its search for purity of movement.
—HOLLY MENINO, *THE PONIES ARE TALKING*

• • •

If you ride, drive, or handle a horse at even the most basic level of interaction, you are contributing to the horse's training.
—SARAH BLANCHARD, *THE POWER OF POSITIVE HORSE TRAINING*

• • •

To practice equestrian art is to establish a conversation on a higher level with the horse; a dialogue of courtesy and finesse.
—NUNO OLIVEIRA

• • •

I've found that my most successful horses . . . all have certain traits in common. They're all very brave, good movers and solid individual jumping, with the boldness to attack the cross-country courses.
—MIKE HUBER

• • •

Movement is the basis of our communication with horses. . . .
—HOLLY MENINO, *THE PONIES ARE TALKING*

• • •

If your horse says no, you either asked the wrong question, or
asked the question wrong.
—PAT PARELLI

• • •

A variety of breeds can be mixed together to produce the show
pony. Most often the mixture contains Thoroughbred and pony
breeds.
—COLIN VOGEL, *COMPLETE HORSE CARE MANUAL*

• • •

If you act like you've only got fifteen minutes, it'll take all day.
Act like you've got all day and it'll take fifteen minutes.
—MONTY ROBERTS

• • •

Listen to what the horse is saying to you.
—ADELE MCCORMICK AND MARLENA MCCORMICK,
HORSE SENSE AND THE HUMAN HEART

• • •

Neither should . . . the lessons be for too long a period; they
fatigue and bore a horse, and it should be returned to the stable
with the same good spirits it had upon leaving it.
—FRANÇOIS ROBICHON DE LA GUÉRINIÈRE

• • •

Care, and not fine stables, makes a good horse.
—DANISH PROVERB

• • •

When my horse is running good, I don't stop to give him sugar.
—WILLIAM FAULKNER

• • •

The human is supposed to be the teacher, but a lot of times
maybe the owner of the horse can't ride a swinging gate in a
windstorm. Yet, they are supposed to be this authoritative figure
to the horse and it doesn't work.
—BUCK BRANNAMAN

• • •

Treat a horse like a woman and a woman like a horse. And they'll
both win for you.
—ELIZABETH ARDEN (1878–1966)

• • •

Once the horse bites you, you never get over it.
—PAUL CLEVELAND

• • •

Sudden severe pain in the abdomen in the horse is referred to
as colic.
—JAMES M. GIFFIN, TOM GORE, *HORSE OWNER'S
VETERINARY HANDBOOK*

• • •

A trainer has to be observant. He has to watch the horses and
figure out what they are thinking. This requires a feel for horses.
This feel is directly connected to passion.
—DAVID COLLINS

• • •

You can often tell a horse's age by his teeth.
—DEBORAH BURNS, *STOREY'S HORSE-LOVER'S ENCYCLOPEDIA*

• • •

It's a funny thing, but we always seem to get the horse that teaches us the very thing we need to learn.
—PERRY WOOD, *REAL RIDING: HOW TO RIDE IN HARMONY WITH HORSES*

• • •

I didn't know anything about horses. But I got a job . . . mucking stalls. I lived right with the horses. . . . I fell asleep listening to their nickering and woke up with the smell in my nose.
—CHRIS IRWIN, *HORSES DON'T LIE*

• • •

Confidence is absolutely essential because without it the horse just cannot make a sufficient surrender of himself, mentally and physically, to learn and to absorb our teaching. Mental and physical processes are so intimately connected, that they cannot be separated.
—HENRY WYNMALEN

• • •

During maximal physical exercise, the cardiac output of a racehorse increases to seven times normal while the heart rate increases to 200 beats per minute.
—JAMES M. GIFFIN, TOM GORE, *HORSE OWNER'S VETERINARY HANDBOOK*

• • •

Look again . . . instead of a fighting horse, you see a dancing horse.
—KLAUS FERDINAND HEMPFLING

• • •

When your horse shies at an object and is unwilling to go up to it, he should be shown that there is nothing fearful in it, least of all to a courageous horse like him; but if this fails, touch the object yourself that seems so dreadful to him, and lead him up to it with gentleness.
—XENOPHON

• • •

The name "horse whisperer" appears to be an ancient one from the British Isles, given to people whose rapport with horses seemed almost mystical.
—PAUL TRACHTMAN

• • •

There is something noble about horses that makes us want to treat them well. When we treat horses with the respect they deserve, they provide us with many unique opportunities to find a type of nobility in ourselves as well.
—CHERRY HILL

• • •

Time and patience are required of all good horsemen, so hurry when you are not around your horse.
—BOB DENHARDT

• • •

The Imperial Spanish Riding School in Vienna existed for over two hundred years for the sole purpose of breeding and training their beautiful Leppizan horses and in developing that type of riding known as "Haute Ecole."
—CARL RASWAN, *DRINKERS OF THE WIND*

• • •

A horse can see behind him, up to a point. There's a blind spot directly to the rear and out to about ten feet. If a horse doesn't really trust his rider or is bothered by him, he'll become very insecure every time the rider passes through that blind spot . . .
—BUCK BRANNAMAN

• • •

Bonding is profoundly physical. We learn our horses' body language and they learn to respond to a body language we use—body pressures and positions called aids—to ask for changes in gait and direction.
—MAXINE KUMIN

• • •

Intimate acquaintance with the horse's knowledge and leading the kind of life that entails the continual reimaginings of horse-manship mark the faces of some older riders with the look that I have also seen on the faces of a few poets and thinkers, the incandescent gaze of unmediated awareness that one might be tempted to call innocence . . .
—VICKI HEARNE, *ADAM'S TASK*

• • •

I know the horse too well. I have known the horse in war and in peace, and there is no place where a horse is comfortable. A horse thinks of too many things to do which you do not expect. He is apt to bite you in the leg when you think he is half asleep.
—MARK TWAIN

• • •

Encephalomyelitis is a disease . . . that is spread by blood-sucking insects that transmit the disease from one horse to another; this explains why it is a late summer and fall disease, for it is then that the transporting hosts are most prevalent. It is . . . referred to among horsemen as "sleeping sickness."
—BEN K. GREEN, *SLEEPING SICKNESS*

• • •

A view of the ancestry of the horse provides us a foundation to understand the behavioral biology of the domestic horse . . .
—GEORGE WARING

• • •

For a horse with a solid head, don't try to break it through with a mallet, try to melt it with sugar!
—ANONYMOUS

• • •

When training his horse, the rider must repeat over and over again, "I have time."
—ANONYMOUS

• • •

When selecting your first horse, there is one absolute rule that you should consider sacred. Don't break it under any circumstances, no matter how tempting: Inexperienced riders must not work with inexperienced horses.
—JUDITH DUTSON

• • •

In training there is always the tendency to proceed too rapidly; go slowly with careful, cautious steps. Make frequent demands; be content with little; be lavish in rewards.
—GENERAL FAVEROT DE KERBRECH

• • •

An extra pressure, a silent rebuke, an unseen praising, a firm correction: all these passed between us as through telegraph wires.
—CHRISTILOT HANSON BOYLEN

• • •

When you own a horse, you must give a part of your life to the horse. There will be occasions when you must give up other things you like—such as sleep, warmth, and comfort—to ensure that your horse receives proper care.
—CHERRY HILL

• • •

A good horse trainer can get a horse to do what he wants him to do. A great trainer can get a horse to want to do it.
—MONTY ROBERTS

• • •

A horse is the . . . subject whereupon the art worketh, and is a creature sensible, and . . . so far as he is moved to do anything, he is thereunto moved by sense and feeling . . . this is common to all sensible creatures, to shun all things as annoy them, and to like all such things as do delight them.
—JOHN ASTLEY

• • •

You want to do as little as possible but as much as it takes.
—BUCK BRANNAMAN, ON TRAINING

• • •

Nothing on four legs is quicker than a horse heading back to the barn.
—ANONYMOUS

• • •

Actions of dominance by horses in the herd are always "just." Through body language there is always a warning . . . before an actual strike or bite occurs. That is why . . . recognizing "what happened before what happened happened" is the critical part of the equation in teaching horses.
—PETER FULLER

• • •

They have different personalities . . . much like people do. . . . Until you learn to communicate in their language, you are not likely to effectively deal with their individual needs. When you do . . . horses will work as willingly with man as they do with one another.
—MONTY ROBERTS

• • •

Any horse being treated for a disease that is accompanied by high fever and severe dehydration might get over the disease but die from the exhaustion and malnutrition that had occurred during the time of the most severe part of the sickness.
—BEN K. GREEN, *SLEEPING SICKNESS*

• • •

Burt taught me how to rub down a horse and put the bandages on after a race and steam a horse out and a lot of valuable things for any man to know. He could wrap a bandage on a horse's leg so smooth that if it had been the same color you would think it was his skin . . . .
—SHERWOOD ANDERSON

• • •

To learn all that a horse could teach, was a world of knowledge, but only a beginning.
—MARY O'HARA

• • •

When the horse understands what you want, he will do what that is, right up to the limit of his physical capacity and sometimes well beyond it.
—BILL DORRANCE AND LESLIE DESMOND, *TRUE HORSEMANSHIP THROUGH FEEL*

• • •

Frank Whiteley Jr. is one of the deadliest trainers of first-time starters in the history of racing—a man who wins upward of 40 percent of all such attempts, a man who trains horses like they are put together with Swiss-clockwork efficiency.
—STEVE DAVIDOWITZ

• • •

Almost any sick animal with a raging fever will have the presence of mind or enough instinct to drink, but few if any will eat feed.
—BEN K. GREEN, *SLEEPING SICKNESS*

• • •

The wildest colts make the best horses.
—PLUTARCH

• • •

Hemlock is a deadly poison for humans, but is consumed without ill effect by mice, sheep, goats, and horses. PCP, or angel dust, which drives humans into a frenzy, is used as a sedative for horses.
—DEBORAH GOLDSMITH

• • •

There never was a rider so smart that some horse could not teach him a new trick. Because of this, horsemanship and horse training is a lifelong study.
—PAUL T. ALBERT

• • •

Don't catch your horse, let your horse catch you.
—MONTY ROBERTS

• • •

You can't train a horse with shouts, and expect it to obey a
whisper.
—ANONYMOUS

• • •

Horses are predictably unpredictable.
—GAGE LORETTA

• • •

Ninety-nine percent of all horses have quite a number of bad
habits which are commonly put down to disobedience. And
ninety-nine percent of all riders do not understand how to break
their horses of such habits.
—WILHELM MUSLER, *RIDING LOGIC*

• • •

Thou must learn the thoughts of the noble horse.
—JOHANN WOLFGANG VON GOETHE (1749–1832)

• • •

It is the difficult horses that have the most to give you.
—LENDON GRAY

• • •

You never get the pleasure of owning a horse, you only have the
pleasure of being its slave.
—ANONYMOUS

• • •

We follow the book. If we have a disagreement, we open the book. . . . We have nothing to invent. Everything in this sport has been written down already.
—NELSON PESSOA

• • •

In attempting to develop a satisfactory relationship with a horse, it is enormously useful to understand the animal's vocabulary of pantomime and sound. But truly effective communications depends on matters more fundamental than language.
—TOM AINSLIE, *THE BODY LANGUAGE OF HORSES*

• • •

A horse doesn't care how much you know until he knows how much you care.
—PAT PARELLI

• • •

It takes no more time and effort to train and finish out a good looking horse than a poor looking one.
—DICK SPENCER III

• • •

Horses need care when they are idle as well as when they are actively being trained or ridden. Their needs do not diminish if your interest does.
—CHERRY HILL

• • •

The two outstanding memories in the animal kingdom are the elephant and the horse. In the case of the horse, you have to remember when to run in order to stay alive.
—DR. ROBERT MILLER

• • •

Nanticoke [a show jumper of the 1960s] reinforced a lesson I'd already started to learn from other horses: never try to muscle your way with a horse.
—RODNEY JENKINS

• • •

In training horses, one trains himself.
—ANTOINE DE PLUVINET

• • •

One key to getting along well with a horse is to view him as a fellow creature rather than as for entertainment.
—PATRICIA JACOBSON AND MARCIA HAYES

• • •

A horse's memory outweighs his reasoning ability. It is therefore important not to allow him to develop any bad habits because he is likely to remember them forever.
—TWILA DIAN, *ALL ABOUT HORSES*

• • •

Closeness, friendship, affection: keeping your own horse means all these things.
—BERTRAND LECLAIR

• • •

We dominate a horse by mind over matter. We could never do it by brute strength.
—MONICA DICKENS

• • •

You can't control a young horse unless you can control yourself.
—LINCOLN STEFFANS

• • •

Horses are not tamed by whips or blows. The strength of ten men is not so strong as a single strike of the hoof; the experience of ten men is not enough, for this is the unexpected, the unpredictable.
—BERYL MARKHAM (1902–1986)

• • •

Horses reflect the emotions of their herd mates, thus the emotion of fear can run rampant through the herd like wildfire.
—KELLY MARKS

• • •

Breed the best to the best and hope for the best.
—JOHN MADDEN

• • •

I have thought that to breed a noble horse is to share with God in one of His mysteries.
—TOM LEA, *THE HANDS OF CANTU*

• • •

The horse will leap over trenches, will jump out of them, will do anything else, provided one grants him praise and respite after his accomplishment.
—XENOPHON

• • •

[T]here is a potential for danger when working with large animals.
—SHAWNA KARRASCH

• • •

Dressage's magic formula is the overpowering force of a combination of gentleness and repetition.
—PRINCESS DE LA TOUR D'AUVERGNE

• • •

Thou must learn the thoughts of the noble horse whom thou wouldst ride. Be not indiscreet in thy demands, nor require him to perform indiscreetly.
—JOHANN WOLFGANG VON GOETHE

• • •

Patience is equally necessary in order not to grow immoderately demanding, which always happens when we do not reward an initial compliance by immediate cessation of the demand, but try to enjoy a victory until the horse becomes cross or confused.
—WALDEMAR SEUNIG

• • •

God, grant me the serenity to take in as many horses as possible, the courage to convince my partner this is a good thing, and, the wisdom to know how to accomplish this task.
—HORSE SERENITY PRAYER

• • •

Dressage lessons in the mange, by reason of their constraints on the horse, must be of short duration and the horse must return to the stable in as happy a frame of mind as when he left it.
—GENERAL ALEXIS L'HOTTE

• • •

The Arabs have found out that which the English breeder should never forget, that the female is more concerned than the male in the excellence and value of produce; and the genealogies of their horses are always reckoned from the mothers.
—WILLIAM YOUATT (1776–1847)

• • •

Some people claim that any damn fool can train a racehorse. . . .
—CARL A. NAFZGER, *TRAITS OF A WINNER*

• • •

Those who claim it is "unethical" to ask a horse to do something it would not do of its own inclination are being naive and foolish; but equally naive are those who expect to teach a horse to do their bidding without taking into account its natural inclinations.
—STEPHEN BUDIANSKY, *THE NATURE OF HORSE*

• • •

If your horse doesn't care, you shouldn't either.
—LINSY LEE

• • •

Understanding the instinctive behavior of the wild horse is crucial to our understanding of his domesticated relatives.
—CHERYL KIMBALL, *THE EVERYTHING HORSE BOOK*

• • •

Horses do think. Not very deeply, perhaps, but enough to get you into a lot of trouble.
—PATRICIA JACOBSON AND MARCIA HAYES

• • •

In order to make a horse, one must first create a rider.
—STEPHANIE LILE

• • •

Horses have a phenomenal memory and there's no time lapse. They memorize something that impresses them, good or bad, and ten years go by, it's still there.
—DR. ROBERT MILLER

• • •

It takes all the dignity out of a horse to make him do tricks. Why, a trick horse is kind of like an actor—no dignity, no character of his own.
—JOHN STEINBECK

• • •

Lew wondered if it was true that at the training gallops Charlie always carried two stopwatches, one for other people, showing whatever time he wanted them to see, and one he looked at later on, all by himself. Of course . . . it's true. I wish he was training my horse.
—MAURICE GEE, *THE LOSERS*

• • •

I've spent so many years living and working with them that at times I still feel I understand horses better than humans.
—CHRIS IRWIN AND BOB WEBER, *DANCING WITH YOUR DARK HORSE*

• • •

In order to excel at an art it is not enough to know the principles and to have practiced them for a long time. It is also necessary to be able to choose wisely the subjects that are capable of executing these principles.
—GASPARD DE SAUNIER

• • •

Anticipate problems and correct them before they happen. Controlling the horse's thinking is much easier than trying to control 1,000 pounds. This holds true whether you're on or off the horse, and may be the most important concept you can learn. . . .
—MIKE SMITH, *GETTING THE MOST FROM RIDING LESSONS*

• • •

Disappointment usually awaits beginners who expect to become accomplished horsepeople without experienced horses and without the aid of a professional trainer.
—J. WARREN EVANS

• • •

In a few generations you can breed a racehorse.
—PIERRE-AUGUSTE RENOIR (1841–1919)

• • •

It's a funny thing—the better you get at training, the cleverer your horses become!
—KELLY MARKS

• • •

Sometimes you have to put your foot down to get a leg up.
—DAVE WEINBAUM

• • •

It is the best of lessons if the horse gets a season of repose whenever he has behaved to his rider's satisfaction.
—XENOPHON

• • •

Those Quoted

Abbey, Edward
Adams, John
Ade, George
Adler, C. S.
Aesop,
Ainslie, Tom
Albert, Paul T.
Allen, Dick
Alstad, Ken
Anderson, Chic
Anderson, C.W.
Anderson, M. Paul
Anderson, Sherwood
Andrews, Lynn V.
Anonymous

Arcaro, Eddie
Arden, Elizabeth
Arendt, Hannah
Armstrong, Samantha
Asmussen, Steve
Assante, Armand
Astley, John
Auf der Maur, Melissa
Aurelius, Marcus
Austen, Jane
Avicenna,
Axthelm, Pete
Babel, Isaac
Bagnold, Enid
Balding, Clare

Baldwin, James
Balkenhol, Klaus
Barbier, Dominique
Barich, Bill
Barnes, Simon
Barry, Dave
Baruch, Bernard
Beddoes, Dick
Belloc, Hilaire
Bench, Johnny
Beyer, Andrew
Binding, Rudolf C.
Bixby, Lawrence
Blackmore, Richard
Blake, William

Those Quoted

Dian, Twila
Dickens, Monica
Dickey, John Sloan
Disraeli, Benjamin
Dorrance, Tom
Dostoevsky, Fyodor
Doyle, Sir Arthur
    Conan
Drager, Marvin
Drape, Joe
Duke of Edinburgh
Duncan, Ronald
Dutson, Judith
Dylan, Bob
Dyson, Freeman
Ed, Mr.
Edwards, Gladys
    Brown
Eichberg, Henning
Eliot, George
Elk, Nicholas Black
Engel, Matthew
Erhard, Werner
Estes, J. A.
Evans, Dale
Evans, J. Warren
Evans, Nicholas
Farley, Walter
Faulkner, William
Ferber, Amanda

Fields, W. C.
Filion, Herve
Findlay, Richard
Fisher, Joely
Fitzsimmons, James
Flaherty, Joe
Fogelberg, Dan
Foote, John Taintor
Forbis, Judith
Forsten, Char
Fosdick, Harry
    Emerson
Francis, Dick
Franklin, Benjamin
Frazer, Sir James
    George
Freud, Sigmund
Frost, Robert Lee
Fuller, Thomas
Furst, Elizabeth
Gaffney, Jimmy
Gallegly, Elton
Galsworthy, John
Garretty, Marion C.
Garson, Nona
GaWaNi Pony Boy
Gee, Maurice
Geertz, Clifford
Giffin, James M.
Ginsburg, Debra

Gissing, George
Glass, Andrew
Goethe, Johann
    Wolfgang
Goldsmith, Deborah
Goldsmith, Oliver
Goodnight, Julie
Goodnight, Veryl
Gordon-Watson,
    Mary
Gore, Tom
Goudge, Elizabeth
Gould, Stephen Jay
Gould, Bruce
Grable, Betty
Grant, Ulysses S.
Grant, Jim
Gray, Peter
Gray, Lendon
Green, Ben K.
Greenstreet, Barbara
Gribbin Jr., Emmet
Hall, Donald
Hammond, Gerald
Hansen, Joan
Harbut, Will
Hare, Julius
Harris, Moira C.
Harris, Susan E.
Harrison, Stanley

Those Quoted

L'Hotte, Alexis
Licart, Commandant Jean
Lile, Stephanie
Lincoln, Abraham
Lippmann, Walter
Livingston, Barbara D.
Livingston, Phil
Llewellyn, Col. Sir Harry
Lofting, Hugh
Longmore, Andrew
Longstreet, Augustus B.
Loretta, Gage
Lucas, E.V.
Lukas, D. Wayne
Lyons, John
Mackall, Dandi Daley
MacLeisch, Archibald
Madden, John
Mairinger, Franz
Malo, David
Mankiewicz, Joseph L.
Mannes, Marya
Markham, Beryl
Markham, Gervaise
Marks, Kelly
Marquand, J. P.
Martino, Teresa

Tsimmu
Marx, Groucho
Mauch, Gene
Mayfield, Marvin
Mayne, Kenny
McCaffrey, Anne
McCain, Ginger
McCarthy, Cormac
McClelland, Ted
McClung, Cooky
McCormick, Adele
McCormick, Marlena
McDowall, Roddy
McEvoy, Hallie
McGinniss, Joe
McGuane, Thomas
McHargue, Georgess
McManaman, Steve
McRae, Marlene
McTaggart, M. F.
McWilliams, Peter
Mearns, Dan
Melde, Merri
Melville, Herman
Menino, Holly
Mercer, James
Merz, Robert L.
Miller, Albert G.
Miller, Henry
Miller, Robert

Mitchell, Elizabeth
Mitchell, Jodie
Mitchell, Waddie
Montapert, Alfred A.
Moon, Vicky
Moore, Charlette
Morey, Walt
Morgan, Bert
Morris, George H.
Mortensen, Ky
Moser, Barry
Mullen, C. J. J.
Munchkin, R. W.
Munro, H. H.
Murphy, Dennis
Musler, Wilhelm
Myles, Alannah
Nack, William
Nafzger, Carl A.
Nash, Raymond
Nelson, Willie
Newell, J. Philip
Novoselic, Krist
Nusser, Susan
O'Rourke, P. J.
Oaksey, John
O'Brien, Vincent
O'Connor, Sally
O'Doherty, Ian
O'Hara, Mary

Those Quoted

Smith, Gene
Smith, Mike
Smith, Red
Smith, Tom
Snyder-Smith, Donna
Somerville , E. OE
Soren, Ingrid
Sovey-Nelson, Melissa
Spates, Pete
Spencer III, Dick
Squire, J. C.
Steele, Wilbur Daniel
Steffans, Lincoln
Steinbeck, John
Steinkraus, William
Stendhal, Henri B.
Stone, Sharon
Strickland, Charlene
Sugar, Bert
Summers, Charles
Summers, Rita
Surtees, Robert Smith
Sweczek, Dr. Thomas
Sweet, Ronnie
Swinchart, Spring
Syrus, Publilius
Tadlock, Annamaria
Tafford, Tyler
Tagg, Barclay
Tagore, Rabindranath
Theodorescu, George

Theroux, Phillis
Thomson, James
Thorn, Stephanie M
Thornton, T. D.
Tolstoy, Leo
Trachtman, Paul
Trollope, Anthony
Truscot, Jr., Lt.
   Gen. L.K.
Tse-Tung, Mao
Tuchman, Barbara
Turcotte, Ron
Twain, Mark
Vanderbilt, Victoria
Virgil
Vogel, Colin
Wadsworth,
   William P.
Walker, Stella
Wall, Maryjean
Wallace, Edgar
Walsh, M. Emmet
Walsh, Ruby
Wanless, Mary
Ward, Greg
Waring, George
Warner, Gertrude
   Chandler
Watman, Max
Wayne, John
Weber, Bob

Weinbaum, Dave
Welch, Buster
Welcome, John
Westmark, Jan
White, T. H.
Wiescamp, Harry
Wilhelm, Charles
Williams, Jimmy
Wilson, Earl
Winfrey, Carey
Winn, Matt
Wittgenstein, Ludwig
Wofford, James C.
Wolf, A. London
Wolf, Linda Little
Wolfgang von Goethe,
   Johann
Wood, Perry
Woolfe, Jr., Raymond
Wright, Gordon
Wyatt, Thomas
Wynmalen, Henry
Xenophon
Yeats, William Butler
Youatt, William
Youngman, Henny
Zang, Linda
Zarzyski, Paul
Zito, Nick